Dedication of
The Stuff of Dreams

Other works by Terrence McNally

Plays
And Things That Go Bump in the Night
¡Cuba Si!
Next
Sweet Eros and Witness
Tour in "Collision Course"
Where Has Tommy Flowers Gone?
Whiskey
Bad Habits
The Ritz
It's Only a Play
Frankie and Johnny in the Clair de Lune
Faith, Hope, and Charity
The Lisbon Traviata
Lips Together, Teeth Apart
A Perfect Ganesh
Love! Valour! Compassion!
By the Sea, By the Sea, By the Beautiful Sea
Master Class
Five Short Plays
Corpus Christi
The Wibby, Wobbly, Wiggly Dance That Cleopatterer Did
Full Frontal Nudity
Prelude & Liebestod
The Stendahl Syndrome

Musicals and Operas (librettos)
The Rink
Kiss of the Spider Woman
Ragtime
The Full Monty
The Visit
A Man of No Importance
Dead Man Walking

Screenplays and Teleplays
Apple Pie
The Five Forty-Eight
Mama Malone
Sam Found Out or The Queen of Mababawe (written with Wendy Wasserstein)
Andre's Mother
Trying Times II: L/S/M/F/T
Frankie and Johnny in the Clair de Lune
The Last Mile
Common Ground (Mr. Roberts)
The Ritz
Love! Valour! Compassion!

TERRENCE McNALLY

Dedication or
The Stuff of Dreams

Grove Press
New York

Published simultaneously in Canada
Printed in the United States of America

FIRST EDITION

Library of Congress Cataloging-in-Publication Data

McNally, Terrence.
    Dedication or The stuff of dreams by Terrence McNally.—1st ed.
      p. cm.
    ISBN-10: 0-8021-4245-1
    ISBN-13: 978-0-8021-4245-0
      1. Amateur theater—Drama.   2. New York (State)—Drama.   I. Title: Dedication.
    II. Title: Stuff of dreams.   III. Title.
    PS3563.A323D43 2006
    812'.54—dc22

                                                                                            2005044787

Grove Press
an imprint of Grove/Atlantic, Inc.
841 Broadway
New York, NY 10003

06 07 08 09 10   10 9 8 7 6 5 4 3 2 1

For Marian Seldes

Dedication or The Stuff of Dreams had its world premiere at the Williamstown Theatre Festival in Williamstown, Massachusetts, on August 11, 2004. Michael Ritchie, producer; Deborah Fehr, general manager; and Jenny C. Gersten, associate producer. The cast was as follows:

LOU NUNCLE   Boyd Gaines

JESSIE   Debra Monk

IDA HEAD   Kellie Overby

TOBY CASSIDY   Darren Pettie

ARNOLD CHALK   Larry Pine

ANNABELLE WILLARD   Marian Seldes

EDWARD   R. E. Rodgers

Directed by Scott Ellis
Anna Louizos, set design; William Ivey Long, costume design; Kenneth Posner, lighting design; Eileen Tague, sound design; Matthew Silver, stage manager; Christopher Akins, production manager; and Cindy Tolan, casting.

Dedication or The Stuff of Dreams had its New York City premiere on August 18, 2005, and was produced by Primary Stages. Casey Childs, executive producer; Andrew Leynse, artistic director; Elliot Fox, managing director. Produced in association with Norma Langworthy, Jamie deRoy, and Michael Filerman. The cast was as follows:

LOU NUNCLE   Nathan Lane

JESSIE   Alison Fraser

IDA HEAD   Miriam Shor

TOBY CASSIDY   Darren Pettie

ARNOLD CHALK   Michael Countryman

ANNABELLE WILLARD   Marian Seldes

EDWARD   R. E. Rodgers

Directed by Michael Morris
Narelle Sissons, set design; Laura Crow, costume design; Jeff Croiter, lighting design; Lindsay Jones, original music and sound design; R. Jay Duckworth, props design; Paul Huntley, wig design; B. H. Barry, fight director; Emily N. Wells, production stage manager; Talia Krispel, assistant stage manager; Lester Grant, production manager; Stephanie Klapper, casting; and Tyler Marchant, associate artistic director.

Dedication or
The Stuff of Dreams

CAST

LOU NUNCLE

JESSIE, his partner

IDA HEAD, Jessie's daughter

TOBY CASSIDY, Ida's boyfriend

ARNOLD CHALK

ANNABELLE WILLARD

EDWARD, her driver

The place: a theatre

The time: now

ACT ONE

Darkness. Utter. We don't know where we are.

LOU   Jessie, what's happening? Jessie, where are we? Where have you brought me? This better be good, Jessie.

JESSIE   Hold your horses.

LOU   You sound far away. Where did you go?

JESSIE   I'm right here. Don't try to peek.

LOU   I'm not peeking. Who could peek with this thing on?

JESSIE   I want you to be surprised.

There is a sound.

LOU   Are you all right?

JESSIE   What was that?

LOU   I don't know. I thought it was you. Are you all right?

JESSIE   I'm fine. What was that sound, then? I thought it was you.

LOU   How could it be me? I haven't moved. I thought it was you, banging into something. Are you all right?

JESSIE   I'm fine. How are you?

LOU   I'm fine. Just hurry up!

JESSIE   Oh!

LOU   What happened?

JESSIE   I see what it was.

LOU   What was it?

JESSIE   Never mind, it doesn't matter.

LOU   What do you mean, it doesn't matter? What doesn't matter? If this is a surprise party and a lot of people are going to jump out and yell happy birthday, I'm not going to be very nice. I'm warning you, people, I can hear you out there.

JESSIE   Save your breath, Lou, there's no one here. I learned my lesson when I did that for your fortieth. Half our friends took their presents back, you were so horrible to them. Don't move, I'll be right back.

LOU   Where are you going this time?

JESSIE   I said, don't move.

LOU   Where am I going to go like this?

JESSIE   Shit.

LOU   Now what happened?

JESSIE   They worked yesterday.

LOU   What worked?

JESSIE   The lights. Arnold showed me.

LOU   What lights?

JESSIE   We practiced. It was perfect.

LOU   What are you talking about?

JESSIE   I was trying to turn the lights on. I'm sorry, Lou.

Jessie is lighting her way toward him with a flashlight.
It is the first and only illumination we have seen.

JESSIE *(cont.)*   I had it all planned. It was going to be such a nice surprise.

LOU Just tell me what it was and I'll act surprised.

JESSIE It's not the same thing, you know that.

LOU Can I take this thing off now?

JESSIE Hold the flashlight; I'll do it. When I took the blindfold off, you were supposed to go, "Oh my God, Jessie" and not say anything for a very long time.

The blindfold is off. Lou looks ahead and shines the flashlight to determine his surroundings.

LOU Oh my God, Jessie. I won't say anything for a very long time.

JESSIE Surprised?

LOU Oh my God, Jess. Oh my God. Is this what I think it is?

JESSIE Happy birthday, Lou. Happy, happy birthday.

LOU I'm speechless. This is—! How did you know?

JESSIE You only tell me every time we pass it. "If we could just get in there, even for five minutes."

LOU That was just wishful thinking. How did you pull this off? You're amazing.

JESSIE I wanted you to see it with all the lights on.

LOU (*shining the flashlight everywhere*) It's so much bigger than I thought. One, two, three balconies. This was a real showplace. Look, up there, honey. The workmanship, the detail.

JESSIE I see.

LOU The molding, the stucco work.

7

JESSIE You're always saying, they don't build places like this anymore.

LOU They don't know how. It's all gone: the craftsmen and the materials. I bet the acoustics are—(*testing them*) Hello! Do re me fa so la! Ask not what your country can do for you, but what you can do for your country. Listen to that. They're fantastic! *Ich bin ein Berliner.* Go ahead, Jess, try it yourself.

JESSIE Testing. One, two, three, four . . . Testing, this is a test.

LOU Come on, that's no fun.

JESSIE I can't think of anything.

LOU Stepping onto center stage, the inimitable Jessie Nuncle!

JESSIE (*singing*) "I'm as corny as Kansas in August."

LOU You sound like you're right here.

JESSIE I am right here.

LOU They have such presence. Such. . . . Can acoustics have balls?

JESSIE Anything can have balls.

LOU Was that a dig?

JESSIE No, Lou. Happy birthday.

LOU It sounded like a dig.

JESSIE When it's a dig, you'll know it's a dig. Now happy, happy birthday.

LOU Is this my real present?

8

JESSIE   You're impossible.

LOU   And I thought we were going to have kinky sex for my birthday. When you put on the blindfold, I was waiting for the whips and handcuffs to come out.

All the lights suddenly come on.

LOU *(cont.)*   What the hell is that? Who turned the lights on?

JESSIE   Arnold? Was that you?

LOU   Jesus, Jessie, be careful!

A large trapdoor is open very close to where Lou and Jessie have been standing.

LOU *(cont.)*   We could have been killed. We were standing right next to an open trapdoor.

JESSIE   It wasn't that way yesterday. Someone must have opened it.

LOU   You could have killed us with your goddamn blindfolds and surprises.

JESSIE   I didn't do it on purpose.

LOU   I didn't say you did. Now come away from there.

JESSIE   It's so deep.

LOU   I said come away.

JESSIE   That would be some fall.

LOU   Why do you insist on tormenting me? You know I have a fear of heights.

JESSIE   This isn't heights. This is depths. You can hardly see to the bottom.

LOU Jessie, please! One brush with death a day is enough for me.

JESSIE There weren't any holes in the floor yesterday.

LOU It's not a hole. It's a trap. People went up and down through them on lifts in old plays.

JESSIE I know what a trapdoor is, Lou.

LOU Calling it a hole is like calling a cast album a sound track. It hurts my ears.

JESSIE I'm sorry. (*She comes and stands by him, slipping one arm around his waist and looking out to the auditorium.*) So what do you think of this place, big guy?

LOU I'll tell you when my heart stops pounding. What do you think I think? This is what a theatre should be, not some defunct Payless Shoe store in a strip mall, where if you make too big a gesture you hit one of the lights. This is what our audience at Captain Lou and Miss Jessie's deserves. A real theatre with wing space, flies, an orchestra pit.

JESSIE It's what you deserve, Lou.

LOU When I think of this place just standing here, empty, rotting away, year after year, while people like us are starving.

JESSIE We're not starving, Lou.

LOU Artistically starving. It's immoral. My father was right; there is no God.

JESSIE That sounds like something your father would say.

LOU We were fishing on a lake in New Hampshire on our summer vacation:"There is no God." Out of the blue, just like that, he said it, and we'd caught a lot of fish that day. I was ten years old.

JESSIE   That's a terrible thing to tell a child.

LOU   It caught my attention, that's for sure. I've never forgotten it.

JESSIE   I would never tell a child something like that. I'd let them find out for themself.

LOU   It was just his way of saying life isn't fair. And it isn't. Otherwise . . .

JESSIE   Otherwise what?

LOU   Otherwise, a lot of things. We'd own this theatre, you'd be happily married.

JESSIE   I am happy.

LOU   We wouldn't have to do *The Velveteen Rabbit* every two years. Stuff like that.

ARNOLD   (*from below*)   Hello!

JESSIE   Arnold? Is that you down there?

ARNOLD'S VOICE   Are you up there, Jess?

JESSIE   Yes. So is Lou. What are you doing down there?

ARNOLD'S VOICE   I fixed the lights. I'll be right up!

LOU   What's *he* doing here?

JESSIE   We're lucky he is. We'd still be in the dark. Thank you, Arnold!

ARNOLD'S VOICE   It's amazing down here!

JESSIE   Be careful down there!

ARNOLD'S VOICE   There's lots of animal traps down here. They must have a lot of vermin.

JESSIE   Well, don't bring anything up with you.

ARNOLD'S VOICE   Does that sound like something I would do, Jess?

JESSIE   As a matter of fact, it does.

LOU   I thought we were on our own for a change.

JESSIE   We are. What is that supposed to mean?

LOU   Why isn't he at work?

JESSIE   It's Saturday. Someone had to get the lights on and it wasn't going to be me or you.

LOU   If you'd nearly been electrocuted working an antiquated light board in a leaky theatre on Cape Cod during the first act finale of *Pippin* one rainy matinee, you would have developed a healthy respect for electricity yourself. I ended up in the hospital at Hyannisport with Rose Kennedy trying to convert me.

JESSIE   You wish it was Rose Kennedy. It was a nun with a mustache.

LOU   It should have been Jackie.

JESSIE   I remember that performance vividly. I almost ended up in the hospital with you. I was on stage dancing with one leg over my head when all the lights went out. We did the second act with flashlights. God, those were the days.

LOU   Summer stock, yeah!

JESSIE   No, when I could get one leg over my head. I went to visit you between shows, remember?

LOU   I remember. They thought you were my girlfriend.

JESSIE   I hardly knew you. I almost didn't make it back to the theatre, you had me laughing so hard.

LOU   The show really does go on without us, doesn't it?

JESSIE   I think that's very comforting.

LOU   It's very humbling.

JESSIE   Happy, happy, happy birthday, Lou. You like?

LOU   I like, I like all right, Jess. Give me a real theatre like this and I'd bite off live chicken heads and worship Satan eight shows a week. I'd even do *Annie*. A theatre! A theatre! My artistic convictions for a theatre!

JESSIE   How could I not love this man?

LOU   Who says you shouldn't?

JESSIE   I didn't say that. I love you, Lou.

LOU   I love you, too. What did you mean by it?

JESSIE   How could I not love a man who'd bite off live chicken heads to have his own theatre? I find that very romantic. Other women probably wouldn't.

LOU   You think I'm kidding? I'd bite off *your* head.

JESSIE   I know you would. What are you doing down there, Arnold?

ARNOLD'S VOICE   I'll be right up!

JESSIE   Now, be nice.

LOU   I'm always nice.

JESSIE   He worked very hard to get the lights on.

LOU   Actually, I liked it better with them off.

JESSIE   You're impossible.

LOU   Electricity's what killed the theatre. Think about it: The ancient Greeks, the Elizabethans, medieval mystery plays—none of them had electricity and it's been downhill ever since.

JESSIE   Neither will Captain Lou's if we don't pay our utilities by Friday.

LOU   I thought you got an extension?

JESSIE   I did. Don't panic.

LOU   Thanks, honey.

JESSIE   I promised the woman two pairs for Saturday.

LOU   Two pairs? Not comps?

JESSIE   Yes, comps. I couldn't very well ask her to pay for them.

LOU   Jesus, Jessie, that's our best house, Saturday!

JESSIE   I was in no position to negotiate.

LOU   I take it back what I said about electricity. Comps are what's killing the theatre. No one ever asked Aeschylus for comps. Starting tonight, I don't care if a kid has leukemia and he's in a wheelchair—the little bastard pays.

JESSIE   Don't look at me, you're the softy.

ARNOLD *enters from below.*

ARNOLD   I had a hunch yesterday those old fuses wouldn't hold.

JESSIE   Thank God you came by. We were completely in the dark.

ARNOLD Happy birthday, Lou.

He hands him what looks like an old dirty towel.

LOU What is it?

ARNOLD Guess.

LOU A dirty towel.

ARNOLD It was Sophie Tucker's makeup towel. I found it in one of the dressing rooms, in front of the mirror, right where she left it. That towel is the last of the Last of the Red-Hot Mamas.

LOU Look, Jess, her name: Sophie Tucker.

JESSIE My grandparents loved her.

ARNOLD This theatre was a vaudeville house, too. It's been everything. I found a podium down there that could have been used by Charles Dickens or Oscar Wilde. It's a fact both men stood on this very stage and spoke to the people of this town on their American lecture tours.

LOU I'll trade you Sophie Tucker's towel for Oscar Wilde's podium.

JESSIE You will not! We're keeping this.

ARNOLD Who do you think built this place and when, Lou? A robber baron for his showgirl mistress? J. P. Morgan in a random act of municipal beneficence? Daisy Shubert, one of the little known Shubert sisters? Who else played here? The Divine Sarah? Houdini himself? Right where you're standing, I wager Edwin Booth stood —"Friends, Romans, countrymen" —and a mesmerized audience lent him their ears. This is your history, America. Why are you so careless with it?

LOU If you're so unhappy in this country . . .

ARNOLD I'm very happy in this country. That's not what I said.

JESSIE That's not what he said, Lou. Where are you going, Arnold?

ARNOLD There's a locked steamer trunk in another one of the dressing rooms I'm pretty sure belonged to Eugene O'Neill's father.

LOU James O'Neill, the actor?

ARNOLD It's got "Mr. O'Neill—Count of Monte Cristo Company—Deliver to Theatre" stenciled on it. Who else could it belong to? I'm going to open it.

He goes.

JESSIE Sometimes I think Arnold loves the theatre almost as much as you do.

LOU No he doesn't.

JESSIE I said almost.

LOU How did you two get us in here anyway?

JESSIE I just asked. Arnold had nothing to do with it.

LOU What do you mean, you just asked?

JESSIE I spoke to her.

LOU Mrs. Willard? Mrs. Annabelle Willard? You spoke to her?

JESSIE Yes.

LOU What did you do?

JESSIE I just went up to her and asked.

LOU   Where was this? Where do you know Mrs. Willard from?

JESSIE   We were both at the movies.

LOU   What one?

JESSIE   I don't remember.

LOU   How could you forget something like the name of a movie?

JESSIE   I knew you were going to ask that. I don't know, Lou, *Gone with the Wind*.

LOU   *Gone with the Wind*!

JESSIE   I don't remember the name of the goddamn movie.

LOU   Do you remember who was in it?

JESSIE   No!

LOU   Why are you getting so angry?

JESSIE   You do this to me all the time.

LOU   Ask a simple question like the name of a movie?

JESSIE   I don't want to fight.

LOU   Neither do I. Finish your story.

JESSIE   Never mind now.

LOU   You were at the movies watching *Gone with the Wind*.

JESSIE   It wasn't *Gone with the Wind*.

LOU   I don't care anymore.

JESSIE   All right, there I was, watching *Birth of a Nation*.

LOU   Have it your way, Jessie.

JESSIE   And she was in the balcony. A couple of rows in front of me. She was with her driver. It was a matinee. Another rainy matinee. I'd stayed home from work with a headache. It was just the three of us up there. The driver was in the row behind her with a thermos of martinis. Every so often, she would just hold her glass up and he would fill it from behind. Not a word was spoken. She would just hold the glass up and he would just lean forward and pour. He even dropped a couple of pearl onions in. All the time, she never took her eyes from the screen. You got the impression this was a well-rehearsed routine; this is how she always went to the movies. She watched and drank; the chauffeur waited and poured.

LOU   I'd like to see her pull that stunt at Captain Lou's.

JESSIE   Somehow I don't think Captain Lou and Miss Jessie's Magic Theatre for Children of All Ages is on Annabelle Willard's radar screen.

LOU   Maybe it would be if we started serving martinis. "What'll you have this afternoon, little Tiffany?" "I'll take a Stoly martini straight-up, Captain Lou."

JESSIE   I assume they were martinis from the shape of the glass and the fact the liquid was clear, which ruled out Manhattans.

LOU   Nancy Drew *manqué!* I'm impressed. Was Arnold with you?

JESSIE   Of course not. What would I be doing at the movies with Arnold? Anyway, I couldn't concentrate on the movie. I might never be so close to her again; this was my big chance. When the movie ended and the lights came up, I made my move. I went right up to her. The driver looked terrified, like I was a presidential assassin or something. I told her who I was, your wife, how it was your birthday, all you'd done for the community, and couldn't we just have a look around her theatre?

LOU   And she said yes?

JESSIE   It wasn't easy. She said she wasn't insured, what if you fell into the orchestra pit and broke your neck? I promised her we wouldn't sue if you did and she said everyone said that, so I ended up telling her you had cancer and didn't have long to live.

LOU   That's not funny.

JESSIE   I know.

LOU   Jesus, what a thing to tell someone.

JESSIE   I could see I wasn't getting anywhere with her. The driver was starting to hustle her out of there and then, almost as an afterthought, she said she wouldn't be around much longer, that she was dying of cancer and after that she wouldn't care what happened or who broke their neck, and couldn't we just wait? And I said—more as a bonding thing than a deliberate lie—I told her that my husband was dying of cancer, too, that he didn't have much time left to see anything, including her theatre. She asked what kind of cancer and I said of the esophagus.

LOU   The esophagus!

JESSIE   Well, I couldn't very well say I didn't know. Esophagus was the first kind that popped into my mind.

LOU   That's what your mother had. It's what killed her.

JESSIE That's probably why I thought of it. If she asked any questions I would be able to come up with some kind of answer. It's what she has, too.

LOU Who?

JESSIE Mrs. Willard. You don't listen!

LOU Mrs. Willard has cancer of the esophagus?

JESSIE Just like my mom.

LOU And now me.

JESSIE Except you really don't and my mother really did. You just have pretend-cancer of the esophagus. Are you mad?

LOU I'm very mad. Why me? Why didn't you tell her *you* had cancer of the esophagus?

JESSIE I don't know, you sprang to mind. I'll tell her I made a mistake. I said the wrong person had cancer. I'm sorry. Happy birthday, Lou.

LOU How long have I got?

JESSIE That's not funny.

LOU I meant in here.

JESSIE As long as you want.

LOU Your heart was in the right place. It usually is.

JESSIE So is yours.

LOU And a lot of good it's done us.

JESSIE Lou!

LOU We've come a long way, baby. I just wonder if it was in the right direction. Sometimes I feel like such a failure.

JESSIE How can you say that? We've made a wonderful life for ourselves up here.

LOU In a town that neither appreciates or deserves us.

JESSIE Do you want to go back?

LOU What for? That party's over, for the likes of us anyway.

JESSIE I appreciate you, Lou.

LOU Thank you.

JESSIE I wonder what they're going to do with this place when she's gone?

LOU You can be sure it'll be something nobody needs. Another Rite Aid or a Starbucks.

JESSIE Such a great location, too. Right on Main Street.

LOU Dream on, Jessie.

JESSIE Maybe if you just talked to her.

LOU (*in a horribly raspy voice*) "Please give us your theatre, Mrs. Willard."

JESSIE You're so passionate.

LOU "I want to do one last production of *Jack and the Beanstalk* before I croak."

JESSIE If anyone could do it, Lou . . . !

Arnold returns from below. He has a large feather fan.

ARNOLD Look what I found. I think Mr. O'Neill was a cross-dresser. The Count of Monte Cristo onstage, the

Countess of Monte Cristo off! (*He strikes a pose.*) "Once more unto the Breach, deare friends, once more; Or close the Wall up with our English dead: Follow your Spirit; and upon this Charge, Cry, God for Harry, England and Saint George." I could never be an actor. I don't know how you two go out there and do it every night.

LOU   We usually have better material to work with: *Old King Cole, Little Red Riding Hood.*

ARNOLD   That was Shakespeare, Lou. *Henry V.*

JESSIE   He knows it was Shakespeare. Don't get him started.

LOU   I hate Shakespeare. I don't know anyone who's honest who doesn't. In the first place, there's too many words. He said so himself: "Words, words, words." And what are they talking about? "Speak English," I want to yell at the actors. No, instead you get yada yada yada in iambic pentameter for six and a half hours. And the plots! People getting murdered because they lost a handkerchief. Women playing men and no one notices. 'What's with the high voice, buddy? And what are those, pray tell, oh shepherd youth? Look like hooters to me." The plays are so confusing people don't even know what period to set them in. The Scottish Play on the North Pole in 3005—I'm sorry, I'm very confused. I don't deny Shakespeare wrote a lot of great lines. "To be or not to be." "*Et tu*, Brute?" "Let's kill all the lawyers." It's just the goddamn plays you have to sit through to get to them! *King Lear* or *Dumbo,* there's no contest.

JESSIE   He's being outrageous, Arnold. Ignore him.

Arnold has another surprise for Lou.

ARNOLD I bet you never saw one of these before, Lou.

Arnold has uncovered a wind machine apparatus.

ARNOLD (*cont.*) It's a wind machine. It doesn't make real wind . . .

LOU Well, I certainly hope not!

ARNOLD . . . just the sound of wind. The actors have to do the rest. They have to act the wind. Show him, Jess.

Arnold starts turning the crank of the wind machine. It makes quite a racket. Jessie starts acting as if she were being blown about in a violent windstorm. She spins in circles as Arnold cranks faster and faster.

ARNOLD (*cont.*) Yesterday Jessie was flying around the stage like she was Eliza Crossing the Ice in *Uncle Tom's Cabin*. Simon Legree's dogs were nipping at her heels.

He is cranking faster and faster.

JESSIE That's enough, Arnold, stop! You'll give yourself another heart attack.

Arnold stops cranking. Sounds of wind fade away. Silence.

JESSIE (*cont.*) Are you all right?

ARNOLD (*breathing heavily*) You missed quite a performance, Lou.

LOU I'm sure I did.

JESSIE Are you all right?

ARNOLD I'm fine, Jessie; quit fussing. Did you see this trap with the lift, Lou?

LOU Thanks to Jessie, I nearly fell into it.

ARNOLD   I could give you such a production of *Cinderella* if we had one of these at Captain Lou's. Imagine, Jess: The Fairy Godmother conjuring the Pumpkin Coach with her wand and oh-my-God up it comes! A rather small coach, to be sure, but a coach as-if-by-magic, all the same.

JESSIE   The kids would go crazy.

ARNOLD   And then, in the last scene: Prince Charming himself holding the glass slipper on a red velvet pillow! (*He gets down on one knee.*) "I have found my true love. Will you marry me?"

JESSIE   We need a lift, Lou.

LOU   Where are we gonna put one? Who's going to pay for it?

ARNOLD   The first play I ever saw had *two* lifts. *Peter Pan.* Captain Hook and his hardies were on one lift, Peter was on the other. You should have seen us kids.

JESSIE   I bet you were all screaming.

ARNOLD   No, Jess, we were dumbstruck. You could have heard a pin drop up there in The Gods.

JESSIE   The Gods?

ARNOLD   That's what we called the highest balcony, The Gods.

JESSIE   I love that, The Gods! Are you hearing this, Lou?

ARNOLD   This was in Newcastle, the Theatre Royal.

LOU   Of course it was. Everything is better in the English theatre.

ARNOLD   I didn't say that, Lou.

JESSIE   He didn't say that.

LOU   If this were England, we'd be doing pantos, and we'd get big government subsidies, and we'd have *twenty* traps. I'd be the Panto Dame, playing mean old ladies, and Jessie would be Best Boy and get the girl at the end.

ARNOLD   I was talking about *Peter Pan,* which isn't a panto, as a matter of fact, Lou, and only *two* traps at our theatre in Newcastle.

LOU   *Peter Pan* doesn't need two traps. Traps are for villains. Only villains make their entrance from below. A stage trap represents the bowels of the earth, where evil and depravity live. Peter Pan enters through a window because he is all, a creature of good. Captain Hook enters from the basement because he is a son of a bitch.

JESSIE   I'm very glad we're not doing Peter Pan this season. I had no idea it was so unsuitable for children.

ARNOLD   What got into you?

LOU   Nothing got into me. It's my birthday. I get to be like this all day.

ARNOLD   Pissy.

LOU   This isn't pissy. I don't know what it is, but it isn't pissy.

ARNOLD   You want to see something that will cheer you up?

LOU   I don't need cheering up.

ARNOLD   You won't believe what they have in the basement. Costumes, props, stage apparatus—all just rotting away. Some of it's in pretty good nick, though, all things considered. Jess, that Chinese dragon's head we were looking at wasn't papier-mâché. It's real silk.

JESSIE I knew we should've taken it! This time, we are.

ARNOLD You'll think you've died and gone to heaven, Lou.

LOU You've already been down there?

JESSIE Yesterday, I told you. Come on.

LOU Not with my allergies.

JESSIE What allergies?

LOU I'm allergic to stage dust.

JESSIE Since when?

LOU Since Peter Pan.

ARNOLD You don't know what you're missing.

LOU I'll take your word for it.

ARNOLD In Newcastle, we call that pissy, mate.

Arnold and Jessie go beneath the stage.

LOU (*calling after them*) I'm sure there are rats down there! He said there were traps!

The trapdoor closes, cutting him off.

LOU (*cont.*) So, here I am, center stage, solus, on a real stage in a real theatre. A stage and theatre that by rights should belong to me and not some alcoholic millionaire who is letting it go beyond all repair or reason. By what rights is it mine? Divine rights, artistic rights, moral ones. Not that they count for much in these impoverished times when wealth equals good and big equals better. I would transform this shabby, forgotten, forlorn room into a place of wonder and imagination again. That chandelier would sparkle anew if I had to polish every crystal myself. The aisles would be

26

newly carpeted in a gesture of welcome and respect. Those rows of broken seats would be reclaimed in a plush red velvet that said, "Sit down, children, you are safe here. We are going to take you on a wonderful journey to China or Persia or Timbuktu." Today we are going to tell you the amazing story of your favorite character, anyone you choose. But before we begin, there are a few rules, so listen up. I said listen up, you kids in the balcony. That means you, too. No kicking the seat in front of you. No paper airplanes or spitballs. No putting chewing gum under the arms or seat of your chair. No talking, unless the action becomes so unbearably exciting that you have to call out: "Turn around, Robin Hood, quick, the Sheriff is going to kill you." Or so sad that you won't be able to live if you don't speak up. It's up to you that Tinker Bell doesn't die, that Abraham doesn't sacrifice his firstborn. For the precious time that you are here and we actors are before you, the future of the world is in your hands, the fate of the human race is yours to decide. Think about it. The possibilities are boundless, the responsibility is yours. And don't forget to breathe! I know, we all forget to sometimes in the theatre. Me, too. I also stop breathing, it's so wonderful. (*He takes in a deep breath, then lets it out.*) And always the curtain will fall, the story will have ended, and we actors will take our bows. Houselights up! It's over. We can all go home now. But something has changed. Tinker Bell has lived. Cinderella has found her Prince. You will go back to your real world and it will still be raw and painful, ugly even, but maybe a little less so because of what you have seen here today. Harmony and happiness *were* possible. And I will go back to my real world and it, too, will be a little more bearable, a little less unbearable because of what I have given you—and in giving you, have given myself: love and laughter, which are a good deal more nourishing at your age than bread and games. Hell, at *any* age. You lucky, lucky children. When I was your age, I didn't have a theatre in my life. I had to invent one of my own. All I had was a mirror, my mother's closet, and my music.

Strains of Tchaikovsky's Sleeping Beauty.

LOU (*cont.*) I'm telling you a secret now. A secret no one knows but you—not even Jessie, and I tell her everything. Well, almost everything. I would go to my mother's closet and take out her fullest skirt. I would put on the music I loved the best, the *Sleeping Beauty*—it was a waltz—and start to twirl in front of the mirror. Slow, slow I'd twirl, in-a-trance-kind-of-slow. For hours sometimes. It felt like forever.

IDA (*from the back of the house*) Don't fall off the stage, Lou!

LOU Who's there?

IDA (*coming forward*) There isn't a mosh pit. No one's gonna catch you.

LOU Ida?

IDA They told us you were here. I should have guessed. A theatre! Where else? How you doing, Lou?

LOU I'm fine, but your mother is going to be in shock.

IDA Good, I wanted to surprise her. The prodigal daughter come in out of the rain.

LOU It's raining? I left the windows open.

IDA No, it's not raining. You gotta keep up, Lou. You wanna give me a hand?

He helps her onto the stage.

LOU You look good, Ida.

IDA I think you mean rested. Six weeks in rehab will do that for you. (*She takes in the theatre.*) Wow! This must have been quite the place in its day.

LOU They say Duse closed it with *Lady from the Sea.*

IDA I take it that's a person and not a band.

LOU A great Italian actress. Before your time. Before my time, too, actually.

IDA And you still remember her?

LOU No, but people who saw her remembered her—they say she had very expressive hands—and told younger people, and now I'm telling you.

IDA Whoa! She must have been pretty good—or at least her hands were. Duse!

LOU Eleonora Duse.

IDA I'll have her Googled.

TOBY (*from the back of the theatre*) Yo! Ida! What's happening, man?

IDA Nothing's happening. You get my Perrier?

TOBY They only had Poland Spring.

IDA Fuck.

TOBY This is upstate, Eye! They drink tap water. They're normal people. You're lucky they had Poland Spring.

IDA Fuck. Did you tell them it was for Ida Head?

TOBY You're being a bitch.

IDA Ida Head *is* a bitch.

He goes.

IDA (*cont.*) That was a joke.

LOU I hope he got it.

IDA Toby's my soundman. He's the best in the business. Without him, I'd sound like shit. I'm giving a concert in—

LOU That's right, you're opening that new arena. We read all about it. How many does it seat?

IDA Fifty thousand? We're sold out, all five shows.

LOU Your mother and I are in the wrong business. We just did an unauthorized production of *The Lion King* but Disney closed us down, the greedy bastards.

IDA I'd like to patch things up between us.

LOU She'd like that, Ida. The last time you two saw each other was Seattle, right?

IDA The *Panic Attack* tour.

LOU I wanted to come with her that trip—I love Seattle—but we were trying to get *Sinbad the Sailor* up and running. That was a big show for us—all those cutlasses.

IDA You're lucky you didn't. We had such a fight about my father. The name says it all. You'd have to be insane to marry someone named Dirk Head. And then have a child with him.

LOU Insane or in love.

IDA She was always a woman who did what she wanted.

LOU She still is.

IDA I know it couldn't have been easy raising a kid like me. I think I had my first joint in the third grade. By high school, I was completely out of control. I stole one of her paychecks and was on the West Coast the same day. Clueless in San Francisco.

LOU How old were you?

IDA Sixteen. I was in a hurry to find out who I was.

LOU Did you?

IDA How angry I was.

LOU Everybody is angry when they're sixteen. Wait'll you're my age. Then you're really pissed off.

TOBY (*from the back of the theatre*) Yo! Ida! They had everything but Perrier!

IDA Fine.

TOBY But I got you one of everything else, some I never even heard of. And they had these really cool jelly beans in a big glass jar. I took all the licorice ones I could for you. And I got a bag of Red Hots for me. (*He bounds easily onto the stage with a large selection of bottled waters—no helping hand for Toby.*) So are we going to meet your mother and her friend or what?

IDA This is her friend. This is Toby, Lou.

LOU Hello, Toby.

TOBY Hi. You got a Starbucks?

LOU I beg your pardon?

TOBY Does this town have a Starbucks? I need a latte.

LOU   I'm afraid not.

TOBY   Fuck.

LOU   There's a little deli just down the street that makes a decent cup of coffee.

TOBY   Fuck. (*He jumps off the stage and heads up the aisle of the theatre.*)

LOU   Turn left. It's next to the shoe repair.

IDA   Bring me a Kit Kat!

TOBY   Fuck.

He is gone.

LOU   I don't think he heard us.

IDA   Do you think Mom will like him?

LOU   He said three words: Yo, fuck, and Starbucks.

IDA   We've got this whole master/slave S&M thing going. You ever have anyone put clothespins on your nipples?

LOU   Not that I remember.

IDA   It isn't for everyone. He—

LOU   Please!

IDA   You don't even know what I was going to say.

Jessie is heard singing from below the stage.

IDA (*cont.*)   I'm suddenly getting cold feet.

LOU   You'll be fine.

IDA   How do I look?

LOU She'll be so happy to see you.

Jessie enters from below the stage. She is wearing an old costume and a tiara. She carries a wand. She looks fairly ridiculous. Arnold is with her.

JESSIE Thank you, children, thank you. That was "*Je suis Titania*" from the French opera comique *Mignon* by Ambroise Thomas. I used to sing that aria in music school. So did Julie Andrews when she was a child performer in London music halls. It means, "I am Titania, queen of the fairies!"

IDA Hey, Mom.

JESSIE Ida?

IDA How are you?

JESSIE I'm . . . I'm speechless. What are you doing here? Lou!

LOU We've been talking.

JESSIE How long have you been here? Arnold and I were just fooling around in the basement.

LOU I certainly hope not, Arnold.

JESSIE Arnold, this is my daughter, Ida. Arnold's our TD, our technical director.

IDA I know what a TD is, Ma.

ARNOLD I've heard a lot about you from your mom. My two boys are big fans.

JESSIE We found this in wardrobe. It's from *Iolanthe*. Your mother never saw a costume she didn't want to put on.

IDA Could I maybe get a hug or something?

JESSIE Of course you can. I'll give you the biggest hug anybody ever had.

IDA You're not in a play, Ma. Normal size will do.

JESSIE Look at you! Is she beautiful? Is my baby beautiful?

IDA You look good yourself.

JESSIE You don't have to say that.

IDA You do, really. Last time I saw you . . .

JESSIE I was a mess.

IDA I was more of a mess.

JESSIE That's all behind us now.

IDA (*to Arnold*) I was in another rehab. I was climbing the walls. I wasn't fit for human consumption.

ARNOLD As your mother said: It's all behind you now.

IDA I like your hair like that.

JESSIE I like yours, too.

IDA Here, before I forget.

JESSIE Is that what I hope it is?

IDA My new CD.

LOU She won't tell you, but she's got the last one.

JESSIE Of course I'll tell her. I have all your CDs, Ida. I don't always understand them, but I buy them and sometimes I actually listen to them. That was a joke. (*looks at the CD*) *The Curse of a Broken Heart*. It doesn't sound very cheerful but what do I know? I think people should be happy all the time. I like the photo on the cover. Who is it?

IDA Me, through a distorting lens.

JESSIE But you're so much prettier than that.

IDA That's the point! Sadness has melted my features.

JESSIE I'm just an old stick-in-the-mud.

IDA And it's "*an* broken heart."

JESSIE What?

IDA You said "*a* broken heart." Look again. The "an" is the whole point. Everybody has a broken heart. Ida Head has *an* broken heart.

JESSIE Honey, that's just bad grammar. It hurts my ears.

IDA In the music business you gotta be different, Ma. It's dog-eat-dog out there.

LOU So is children's theatre, Ida. Completely vicious.

JESSIE Don't listen to him.

LOU She's used to me by now.

Arnold has started sweeping the stage floor.

JESSIE How did you know we were here? Did you stop by the Dapper Dog?

IDA They told us you were at the old theatre on Main Street.

JESSIE Lou has always wanted to get inside this place, but the owner has always said no. This time I told her it was his birthday.

IDA Happy birthday, Lou.

LOU No, Jessie, you told her I had cancer of the esophagus and *then* she said yes.

35

IDA Oh fuck, Lou. Cancer! Why didn't you tell me?

LOU I don't have cancer of the esophagus. I don't have cancer of anything. Your mother tells these awful lies and gets everybody into trouble.

JESSIE It worked, didn't it? Mrs. Willard has cancer of the esophagus.

ARNOLD Mrs. Willard has cancer of the esophagus?

IDA Who is Mrs. Willard?

JESSIE I don't think she wants it bandied about, Arnold.

LOU Neither do I.

JESSIE You don't have cancer, Lou.

LOU I know that, Jessie, but you told her I did.

JESSIE I told her in confidence, just as she told me. Your secret is safe with her.

LOU What secret? I don't have any secret.

ARNOLD I'm trying to sweep, Jessie—move.

JESSIE Mrs. Willard is the owner. You don't have to do that, Arnold. Arnold hates a dirty theatre.

LOU Arnold hates a dirty anything.

JESSIE When he showed up on our doorstep, we thought an angel had arrived.

ARNOLD A dirty theatre usually means an indifferent production.

JESSIE When Arnold's not toiling away on our behalf, he works at the local nursing home. I'm sure he's indispensable there, too.

36

ARNOLD   I'm not indispensable either place. There's always someone to do what I do.

JESSIE   The difference is: They pay you; we don't.

IDA   You do this for free?

ARNOLD   Your mother and Lou, too.

JESSIE   We do it for love.

IDA   Of what? Of children? The theatre?

LOU   Of everything. Love of everything.

ARNOLD   Good answer, Lou.

TOBY   (*returning*)   Yo! Ida!

LOU   The coffeeman cometh.

TOBY   Okay, here's the scoop. There's gonna be a Starbucks right where the old bank was. We're just six months too early.

IDA   Leave it to Toby. He talks to everyone.

TOBY   And I found out why this place closed.

LOU   It was too big. There wasn't enough audience anymore.

TOBY   No, it was too small for some of the rock 'n' roll acts they were trying to book in here. There wasn't enough room for all their equipment. Ida's show wouldn't fit in here. Neither would her audience.

LOU   I was talking about legit shows.

TOBY   They were before my time. Hi.

IDA   This is her, Toby, this is my mom, the Broadway baby herself.

Toby easily leaps up onto the stage—no helping hand for him.

TOBY   I hope this wasn't too much of a surprise for you, Mrs. Nuncle.

IDA   They're not married.

TOBY   That's cool. Neither are we. Go for it, Ida's mother.

LOU   I said the same thing.

JESSIE   I use Nuncle, but we just never bothered.

TOBY   Nuncle. That's a wild name. Nuncle. What is it?

LOU   I have no idea.

ARNOLD   I think it's Elizabethan. There's a lot of Nuncles in Shakespeare. Hello, I'm Arnold, Arnold Chalk.

JESSIE   Arnold's our technical director.

TOBY   TD! This is so cool. I love people's names. Nuncle, Chalk, Head.

LOU   Do you have a name, Toby?

TOBY   Yes, sir, I do.

LOU   Do you mind sharing it with us?

TOBY   No, sir, I don't. Cassidy, Tobias Starr Cassidy the Third. Starr with two r's, the Third with three Roman numeral I's, all caps. But you can call me Toby.

LOU   We were planning to.

IDA   Toby comes from money and he went to all the best schools but he still wants to rock.

TOBY   I learned more in one year on the road with Ida than all six years at Bard. Here, I brought you a Diet Coke.

IDA I asked for a Kit Kat, too.

TOBY Here's your Kit Kat. Your daughter is a Diet Coke addict. Guzzles 'em morning, noon, and night.

IDA Anything that keeps me off crack.

TOBY She breaks me up, this one.

JESSIE I don't think addiction is a laughing matter.

IDA I'm going to give Toby a sign to hold up: "What you just heard was a joke. You may laugh."

JESSIE Just say something funny and save Toby the trouble.

IDA Zap! What did I tell you, Toby?

TOBY Ida's clean and she's going to stay that way this time. Aren't you, babe?

JESSIE We do read the papers, even up here. It's not like your little missteps went unreported.

IDA That's a good word for them.

LOU Your mother was very upset.

IDA They have visiting days.

TOBY I came. I came every time.

IDA I know you did, Toe.

JESSIE Darling, what was I supposed to do? Go halfway across the country and have them tell me you didn't want to see me?

IDA End of discussion.

LOU I won't have you upsetting your mother.

IDA You don't want to go there, Lou, okay?

LOU Don't cry, Jess. Here.

JESSIE I'm not crying.

TOBY I said to Ida: Babe, you gotta warn people you're coming, especially your folks, but she doesn't listen to me unless we're doing a sound check and then I am like this total god. Okay, Eye, pretend this is a sound check and talk to your mother. It's why we're here.

LOU Arnold, why don't you see if you can find some chairs down there, and take Toby with you.

JESSIE I'm fine. Now stop fussing.

ARNOLD You ever been in the basement of an old theatre, Toby? You're gonna love this. Come with me.

Toby stops at the lift.

TOBY Is that what I think it is?

ARNOLD It's a trapdoor with a lift. "Elevator," you'd call it.

TOBY Ida, this would be so great for the show. You know, during "Crying All the Time Now," you just slowly sink out of view. You're sinking, you're singing, you're sinking, you're singing, you're sinking, you're singing, you're gone. Excellent!

Toby and Arnold are gone.

LOU I want to look at the rest of the place before they kick us out. Your mother's been under a lot of stress lately, Ida.

JESSIE No more stress than usual.

IDA I don't intend to add to it, Lou.

40

LOU Thank you, Ida.

He jumps off the stage with some difficulty and disappears up the aisle toward the back of the house.

IDA Lou's nice.

JESSIE He's been very good to me. We still make each other laugh.

IDA You always liked a man with a good sense of humor. I bet he's a great teacher.

JESSIE His students love him. This year one of them, Billy Lumpke, went all the way to the state finals with a one-man monologue Lou adapted for him from *The Scarlet Letter*. You're smiling.

IDA After all these years, you both still want to be in the theatre!

JESSIE We *are* in the theatre—it's just not one that's going to make us rich or famous or anyone's ever going to read about. Lou calls it T.A.—Theatre Anonymous.

IDA Do you ever miss the other stuff?

JESSIE Oh, sure, honey, how could we not? I hear from some friend in the city who's got a show and I think, "Is that what they're hiring now?" Have I cried myself to sleep? You bet I have.

IDA What's keeping you here?

JESSIE The same thing that brought us: Lou and I are both at a time in our life when the business is just too hard. I think we were both looking for someplace to rest and someone to rest with. It's not the Big Apple here. It's not even a small apple, but it's a good apple. I feel blessed.

IDA Do you ever hear from Dad?

JESSIE No, and I don't expect I ever will.

IDA There was this man who I thought maybe was him. This was a couple of years ago when I was still playing small venues and I could see the audience. The way he kept looking at me. There were tears in his eyes, I'm sure of it. I sent my assistant to ask him to come back but he was gone. I was too chicken to go myself.

JESSIE I bet it was him.

IDA You do?

JESSIE Just a feeling. How could he not want to see you?

IDA He was a bastard.

JESSIE Your father was a handsome bastard.

IDA Most bastards are.

JESSIE I hope Toby's not a bastard.

IDA He treats me like I'm a goddess.

JESSIE Good for you.

IDA And I treat him like shit.

JESSIE Why?

IDA I don't know, I can't help myself. He loves me so much, I get angry sometimes. Have you ever felt that way?

JESSIE No, never. Are you two serious?

IDA He wants to get married.

JESSIE What do *you* want?

IDA I want to stay straight this time.

JESSIE I like your priorities. (*She sniffs.*)

IDA What's the matter?

JESSIE I thought I smelled Mrs. Kagin's cocker spaniel on my top. (*She sniffs again.*) It's not the cocker. It's Mrs. Kagin.

IDA You used to hate dogs. Remember that schnauzer on the third-floor landing at 376? You wanted to poison it.

JESSIE That dog deserved to be poisoned. I don't know, honey. People change. One day I liked dogs. The place was for sale. It seemed like a good idea. I had to do something. Lou was teaching. I've met a lot of very nice people thanks to the Dapper Dog.

IDA It's good to see you.

JESSIE Me too. I was so worried.

IDA It's funny seeing you here.

JESSIE How so?

IDA All those times I waited for you out on the stage after a matinee. The stage manager would turn the ghost light on and I'd think, "What happened? Five minutes ago it was all so pretty." And then you'd come down from the dressing rooms and buy me a hot cocoa at Howard Johnson's before we went home.

JESSIE That Howard Johnson's is gone, honey.

IDA Who was the friend of yours I liked so much? She always had Hershey's Kisses for me? Dottie something.

JESSIE Dottie Riegel. She died, two years ago. She was in a show, too.

43

LOU (*from a distance*)   Can you hear me down there?

JESSIE   Where are you?

LOU   Up here.

JESSIE   Be careful, Lou!

LOU   Fantastic acoustics. I'm barely raising my voice.

JESSIE   Can you hear us?

LOU   Every word. It's a good thing Mrs. Kagin can't.

JESSIE   Don't fall. He's like a child. If he falls and hurts himself . . .

IDA   Nothing's going to happen, Ma.

JESSIE   I don't know what I'd do if anything happened to him.

IDA   Stop worrying.

LOU (*still far away*)   The view is fantastic from up here.

JESSIE   Where are you now?

LOU   At the very top. Can you see me?

JESSIE   I don't want you up there. Come down right now. You're scared of heights, Lou.

LOU   Don't remind me. I'll get dizzy and fall and there won't be a performance of *Aladdin* Saturday morning. Are you ready to catch something? Here it comes!

JESSIE   Don't you dare, Louis Nuncle!

LOU   I'm blowing you a big fat kiss, Miss Jessie.

IDA   Lou, come down, you're scaring her.

LOU You know what you're both acting like, don't you? You're acting like girls!

JESSIE I never said he wasn't a handful.

Arnold and Toby return. They have found a couple of chairs. Also a thunder apparatus; i.e., a thunder sheet.

ARNOLD This is the best we could do. We tried to clean them up.

TOBY It's amazing the stuff they've got down there. It's like a spook house. We found a gallows with a dummy hanging from a rope. It scared the shit out of me.

ARNOLD It was a prop from *Girl of the Golden West,* Act *Five*! I can barely remember when plays were in *three* acts. Everybody wants everything short and sweet now.

JESSIE That's all we need at Captain Lou's, a gallows! We'll be doing horror plays and scaring the kids. Don't tell Lou.

ARNOLD It's not a real gallows.

LOU *(in a box seat now)* What's not a real gallows?

JESSIE Never mind, Lou! He'll want to see if it works.

ARNOLD Wait'll he sees that Roman chariot from *Ben Hur.*

LOU "Romeo, Romeo, wherefore art thou, Romeo."

JESSIE Come down from there, Lou.

LOU Not until you give me my cue.

JESSIE "But soft, what light through yonder window breaks?"

LOU Too many words! Do you like Shakespeare, Toby?

TOBY   Yes, sir, I do, very much. He's my favorite writer.

LOU   You're no fun. You're as bad as Arnold. (*firing an imaginary pistol*) *Sic semper tyrannus!* "Other than that, how did you like the play, Mrs. Lincoln?" I'm on my way.

He is gone.

JESSIE   I haven't heard that Mrs. Lincoln line since Montego Bay when we were asked to leave the cruise ship and Lou and Jessie, the Cosmopolitans, were no more.

IDA   That was a good gig for you.

JESSIE   Cruise ship passengers are either stuffing themselves at another buffet or falling down drunk. The Cosmopolitans were casting their pearls before swine.

ARNOLD   I hope you won't take this the wrong way, Toby, but you don't look like someone who would appreciate Shakespeare.

TOBY   I had an English teacher in high school, Mrs. McElroy—it's all thanks to her. Mrs. Mac taught us Romeo and Juliet were just two young people in love and that we should just feel the words, even if we didn't understand all of them. I mean, what's a fardel?

ARNOLD   I believe a fardel is bound sticks for a bonfire. I know that's not your point, but I happen to know what a fardel is.

TOBY   She had us do scenes from the plays. Sometimes when I'm on my bike and nobody can hear me, I do "To be or not to be." I still remember the Tent Scene from *Julius Caesar.*

ARNOLD You can't forget the Tent Scene. I did it in the sixth form. It must be a good scene for bad actors. Are you any good?

TOBY I'm terrible.

ARNOLD I'm worse.

TOBY No you aren't. "Hah! Portia."

ARNOLD "She is dead!"

TOBY "How scaped I killing when I crossed thee so."

ARNOLD "Hah! Portia."

TOBY "She is dead!"

ARNOLD "How scaped I killing when I crossed thee so."

TOBY "Hah! Portia."

ARNOLD "She is dead."

TOBY "How scaped I killing when I crossed thee so."

JESSIE You both ended up on the right side of the curtain.

Lou is crossing the stage and heading for the wings.

LOU Heads up!

JESSIE What are you doing *now*, Lou?

LOU (*from the wings now*) I want to see if the curtain works.

ARNOLD Let me give you a hand.

JESSIE Leave well enough alone.

The curtain is indeed falling. It is shabby, tattered, and torn.

TOBY Very cool.

ARNOLD   Curtain! Watch yourselves.

The curtain is down. We can hear their muffled voices from behind.

LOU   I don't care what anybody says: There's nothing like a curtain. Who wants to look at an empty stage for twenty minutes before the play begins?

IDA   Rock 'n' roll doesn't need a curtain. You just hit that first chord and pow!

ANNABELLE WILLARD *is seen coming down the center aisle of the theatre.* EDWARD, *her driver, is with her.*

MRS. WILLARD   Gently, gently. You're a sadist, Edward.

ARNOLD   Lou, look over here. There's another curtain and a scrim!

LOU   I want to see that podium of Oscar Wilde's!

ARNOLD   It's in the basement. What about the curtain?

LOU   Leave it down.

Their excited voices fade away as Mrs. Willard and Edward proceed to the stage.

EDWARD   You need morphine.

MRS. WILLARD   Morphine constipates me. It's the worst pain of all. You're trying to pass a block of cement through a very small opening. Have you ever been constipated, Edward?

EDWARD   Not like that, Mrs. Willard.

MRS. WILLARD   You'd probably enjoy it. Now where are these people?

EDWARD   Behind the curtain.

MRS. WILLARD   What are they doing there?

EDWARD   The man brought it down.

MRS. WILLARD   The man? What man?

EDWARD   The man whose birthday it is.

MRS. WILLARD   Ah! I remember now.

EDWARD   Should I bring it up?

MRS. WILLARD   Why bother? They won't stay back there forever. Sooner or later, the curtain always rises. I can wait. I suppose you want to get back to your soaps.

EDWARD   Thank you, Mrs. Willard. It was getting very tense.

MRS. WILLARD   Lift me to the stage first. I can't hop up onto it like the young people. I never could. That's not true either. I never wanted to. I detest people who hop up onto things.

He lifts her onto the stage.

MRS. WILLARD (*cont.*)   Much better. See? I can be nice. Now go.

Edward goes.

MRS. WILLARD (*cont.*)   I'm in a curious mood today. I woke up in one. I had a good night's sleep, too. There is no pain, and what anxiety I feel is generalized, rather than specific. Oh, I still know I am going to die with and of this hideous disease, but not in the next five minutes. For the next five minutes I am mentally and emotionally cancer-free. I should feel wonderful. I should feel happy. No, this mood is something else. This mood is more subtle, more dangerous. It's taking me within myself. I do not wish to be within myself.

This is my question: Why does goodness come so easily to some people and to others not at all? It should be so easy to be good. To be kind, to be generous. Here is the shirt off my back, take it. My heart is yours, it opens itself to you. Goodness should be like breathing: in, out; in, out. Goodness, grace, love. These are the things that should flow ceaselessly from each of us to the other. And so what cosmic life force impedes it? There must be goodness here, in this decaying body, there must be. I would tear my flesh open to find it. I can imagine goodness but I cannot embody it. I can act goodness, pretend it. That's easy for the rich. I write very large checks, even while muttering imprecations against the beneficiaries of my generosity. I detest you, Goodwill Industries, to the tune of ten million dollars. Die, Starving Children, here's twenty million more; suffer, Incurable Diseases and Everyone with a Disability. Take my money and leave me the hell alone.

The curtain behind her begins to rise. At the same time, we hear the voices of the others on the other side.

LOU   There's always that great moment just before the curtain rises. Take it up, Arnold. See what I mean? There will always be a curtain at Captain Lou and Miss Jessie's, if I have to sew and mend it myself. (*Lou turns and sees Mrs. Willard.*) Mrs. Willard.

MRS. WILLARD   I'm not Mrs. Willard.

LOU   I'm sorry.

MRS. WILLARD   I'm what's left of her. But don't stop. I like a man who discourses with passion. The world is entirely too apathetic for my taste. You were discoursing with great passion about the importance of curtains in the theatre.

LOU Like just now: Curtain up and there you were. Who knew you were on the other side? The theatre should surprise us like that. Sneak up on us and go "boo."

MRS. WILLARD Speaking of surprises, you rather spoiled the entrance I had planned for you. Edward!

All eyes follow her gaze up into the theatre flies.

ARNOLD Is that what I think it is?

LOU What is it?

ARNOLD In England, we'd call that a cloudcar.

A cloudcar is slowly lowered from the flies.

LOU A what?

ARNOLD A cloudcar.

MRS. WILLARD Cloudcars were what the gods, magical spirits, or genies traveled in. Usually they crossed the stage at proscenium level but sometimes they descended to the stage. And sometimes—and these were extraordinary circumstances—mere mortals were invited aboard and were lifted up to heaven itself. That would be your apotheosis. I haven't seen a cloudcar put to good use since Baroque theatre and Louis XIV. Modern drama put the kibosh on them.

LOU You're talking about people like Eugene O'Neill or Bernard Shaw, or Ibsen even.

MRS. WILLARD I'm talking about Shakespeare.

LOU But you said modern drama.

MRS. WILLARD   Modern theatre began with Shakespeare. I know when people say it began but they're wrong. Shakespeare put real people on the stage.

TOBY   That's what my high school English teacher always said.

MRS. WILLARD   He didn't need gods and spirits. He trafficked in mere humanity. Cloudcars have been in mothballs ever since.

The others admire the cloudcar.

LOU   That would have been some entrance, Mrs. Willard.

MRS. WILLARD   And an even better exit perhaps. Thank you, Edward. (*She points to the thunder apparatus.*) The thunder apparatus was made in Dublin in 1848. You can still see the artisan's name: Stephen Boyle, Number 14 Moon Street. The wind apparatus came all the way from St. Petersburg. Some tsar's private playhouse, no doubt. Our lovely cloudcar was rescued from a theatre in Norway two weeks before it burned to the ground. Everything else here, I'm told, is American. As are we all, n'est-ce pas?

LOU   Arnold is British.

ARNOLD   But I detest the monarchy and one of these days I'm going to take out United States citizenship.

MRS. WILLARD   You'll have to take a test first. None of my help can pass it. Can you recite the Pledge of Allegiance?

ARNOLD   I was hoping you weren't going to ask me that.

MRS. WILLARD   Neither can I. I can't sing the National Anthem either. I'm surprised they haven't lined us both up and shot us. Now, which one of you is the one with cancer?

LOU I am.

MRS. WILLARD Have you screamed with the pain yet?

LOU No.

MRS. WILLARD You will. Sometimes I wake up in the middle of the night and the only sounds in the house are the clocks—until I interrupt them with my screams. It's very unbecoming.

LOU You've met my wife.

JESSIE At the movies. I told you about my husband and how much he wanted to see your theatre.

MRS. WILLARD I remember. It was a very long film. I got quite drunk.

JESSIE And this is my daughter, Ida, and her friend, Toby, and our colleague, Mr. Chalk.

MRS. WILLARD Hello.

IDA Ida Head.

MRS. WILLARD Come again?

IDA I know. With a name like mine, I should have been in porn. God knows what drugs they were on when they chose it.

MRS. WILLARD Not chemo, that's for certain. Hello, young man.

TOBY Hello, Mrs. Willard.

MRS. WILLARD I like this one. He says just what's necessary and he has a firm handshake. Do you do yard work, Mr. Chalk?

ARNOLD My own, I do.

MRS. WILLARD That doesn't do *me* any good. No one wants to work with their hands anymore. Now where were we?

LOU I believe my wife told you: We run a small, not-for-profit children's theatre.

MRS. WILLARD That's an ugly expression.

LOU Not-for-profit?

MRS. WILLARD Children's theatre. Grown-ups desperately trying to hold the attention of a hostile audience. Where is this torture shop? Why have I never heard of it?

LOU At the Miracle Mall, between the dry cleaner's and Wendy's, Mrs. Willard.

MRS. WILLARD That's why. Location, location, location!

LOU Captain Lou and Miss Jessie's Magic Theatre for Children of All Ages.

MRS. WILLARD That's rather a mouthful for a child, don't you think?

LOU It's preferable to our acronym: C.L.A.M.J.M.T.F.C.O.A.A. Pronounced "Clam-jim-tuf-coe-ah." I'm Captain Lou and my wife is Miss Jessie.

MRS. WILLARD I'm glad we cleared that up.

JESSIE We're doing a children's version of *Cyrano de Bergerac* next month.

MRS. WILLARD Cyrano. He's the one with the nose?

JESSIE You know it?

MRS. WILLARD I detest it. It's a lie. We are never loved for who we really are. We are rejected for who we really are.

LOU I don't agree, Mrs. Willard. *Cyrano* says exactly the opposite: that it is only when people see us as we really are that they can truly love us. And unless we know who we truly are we can never experience the true love of others.

MRS. WILLARD That's quite a plateful for an eight-year-old, don't you think? What's next for the little nippers? *Medea?*

JESSIE She's just playing with you, Lou.

MRS. WILLARD Why not? We're in a theatre. Let's play! Give as good as you get. You want me to hand over my theatre to you? Act like it then.

LOU Who said anything about that?

MRS. WILLARD (*calling off*) Edward!

JESSIE I did, Lou. I thought if you just stated our case.

LOU I wish you'd given me a heads-up.

Edward enters with a martini glass and silver cocktail shaker. He hands her the glass and fills it from behind, just as Jessie described.

ARNOLD They're both too modest to say this, Mrs. Willard, but no one has served this community more selflessly than Lou and Jessie Nuncle. Their sacrifice and dedication to quality children's theatre have never been properly acknowledged. Imagine how your theatre could serve our community.

MRS. WILLARD I'm not interested in serving the community. What has the community ever done for me? You know that ridiculous bumper sticker? "Save the Whales?" I say, "*Eat* the Whales." What has a whale ever done for me?

ARNOLD   I'm talking about the next generation, Mrs. Willard. We have a responsibility to them. If we fail it, we will have failed at everything.

MRS. WILLARD   Did I miss something? I thought we were talking about a piece of real estate and it turns out it was Armageddon. This belief in the theatre. It's like rampant mad cow disease.

She lifts her martini glass. Edward refills it from behind.

ARNOLD   I have two boys. Their mother left us. Without Captain Lou's, I don't know what we would have done. My boys or me. We each found something there, something precious.

MRS. WILLARD   Please don't tug at my heartstrings, Mr. Chalk. It only makes me more irritable than I already am. Thank you, Edward.

LOU   I think what Arnold is trying to say, Mrs. Willard—

ARNOLD   She knows what I'm trying to say, Lou. She just doesn't want to hear it. She'd rather sit here in her empty, decaying theatre with her untold millions, drinking martinis, doing nothing for anyone.

MRS. WILLARD   Most people would if they had the choice.

JESSIE   Never mind, Arnold.

TOBY   This is heavy, Eye!

IDA   I'm going to make her an offer on the place.

ARNOLD   People like you deserve to perish from this earth.

MRS. WILLARD   You'll have your wish very soon, Mr. Chalk.

ARNOLD Unfortunately, you will take the rest of us with you. Your utter indifference to making this a better world for anyone else is an obscenity.

MRS. WILLARD My cancer is the obscenity.

ARNOLD People like you make me want to overthrow governments. You make me want to smash things. You make me wish I'd never come to this country. In England, we have a class system as an excuse for people like you. In this country, there's none. I hate people like you. You have no reason to exist. None. (*to the others*) I'll be next door at Chat 'n' Chew.

MRS. WILLARD They make a lousy martini.

Arnold is gone.

JESSIE Arnold is a socialist, Mrs. Willard.

MRS. WILLARD I would be, too, if I didn't have money. Who's next to abuse the old lady? We haven't heard much from the younger generation.

IDA I'd like to make an offer to buy this place for my mom, Mrs. Willard. She hasn't had an easy life.

JESSIE I never said that, Mrs. Willard.

MRS. WILLARD You didn't have to, Jessie. I could tell just by looking at you. It broke my heart.

IDA I've been a terrible daughter and I want to make it up to her. A place like this would make her and Lou beyond happy. It would be their dreams come true. I'm a singer. A very successful one. I have a lot of money and I am one hundred percent prepared to meet any reasonable price.

MRS. WILLARD I'm not a reasonable woman. Two billion dollars.

IDA Seriously, I'll give you five million dollars for it, as is, which I'm sure is way more than it's worth.

MRS. WILLARD Bargaining for your mother's happiness? I thought love was priceless. All right, *three* billion.

IDA You're a cunt.

MRS. WILLARD Say what?

JESSIE Ida!

IDA A cunt.

MRS. WILLARD That's what I thought you said.

IDA You're going to die and no one will give a shit. Come on, Toby; we'll be next door with Arnold, Mom.

She jumps off the stage and heads up the aisle.

TOBY Ida's right. You're not a very nice person, Mrs. Willard. How does someone get to be like you?

MRS. WILLARD You're young, you'll see.

Toby follows Ida up the aisle.

MRS. WILLARD (*cont.*) Two more down, one to go.

JESSIE This was a terrible idea. I'm sorry, Lou.

LOU Mrs. Willard, we don't have that kind of money to buy this place.

MRS. WILLARD No, but I have a proposal for you. Edward, help Mrs. Nuncle off the stage.

LOU I'll go with you.

JESSIE No, stay, listen to her proposition.

LOU She's not going to give it to us.

JESSIE She hasn't said that.

MRS. WILLARD I can hear every word you're saying.

JESSIE I love you so much when you look like that.

She kisses Lou and lets Edward help her off the stage and leaves.

MRS. WILLARD Let me see it, Lou.

LOU What?

MRS. WILLARD That look that makes her love you so much.

LOU Mrs. Willard.

MRS. WILLARD Call me Annabelle. It's a wonderfully louche name, don't you think? It makes me think of moist female sexual organs. Annabelle! No, it's the word "louche" that makes me think of moist female sexual organs. We'll stick with Mrs. Willard.

LOU Can I ask you a stupid question?

MRS. WILLARD I've begun to think all questions are stupid but ask away.

LOU Do you even like the theatre?

MRS. WILLARD That's not a stupid question.

LOU Thank you

MRS. WILLARD It's an irrelevant one.

LOU Don't you ever get tired of having the last word?

MRS. WILLARD Not really.

LOU   Just answer my question.

MRS. WILLARD   When you have as little life left in you as I do, the theatre assumes a position of such thundering unimportance; I can't begin to tell you! What's *your* prognosis?

LOU   You mean?

MRS. WILLARD   I mean, how long are they giving you? Months? A year?

LOU   I don't know. I don't want to know. Ask Jessie. She's the one who talks to the doctors. What's yours?

MRS. WILLARD   Soon. I don't talk to doctors anymore. I listen to my body. What does your body tell you?

LOU   I'm having a good day.

MRS. WILLARD   Wait till you're grateful for a good five minutes. I don't want to give you my theatre if you're going to croak before me.

LOU   It would be in very good hands with Jessie when I'm gone.

MRS. WILLARD   It means so much to you?

LOU   The theatre has been good to us. We want to give something back. We want a child to be able to say, "I was lucky. Where I grew up, there was a playhouse. I went to a play every week. It was thrilling."

MRS. WILLARD   All right.

LOU   All right? All right, what?

MRS. WILLARD   I'll give it to you. And I'll give you the money to bring it back to life. And I'll give you more money to keep it going. I'll give you lots and lots of money. Money problems are boring. I don't want to hear you have money problems when I'm on the other side. The dead do listen, you know, and I will be listening.

LOU Wait a minute. There are strings attached. There have got to be strings attached.

MRS. WILLARD Just two.

LOU Go on.

MRS. WILLARD Fuck me.

LOU All right. What's the other?

MRS. WILLARD Fuck me again.

She bursts into laughter.

LOU That isn't funny.

MRS. WILLARD To you, probably not, but it tickled my fancy.

LOU The theatre is a joke as well, I suppose? You didn't mean a word you said?

MRS. WILLARD Twirl for me, Lou.

LOU Twirl for you?

MRS. WILLARD Like you were a little boy in front of your mother's mirror.

LOU You were watching.

MRS. WILLARD See that little window up there? So there you were: twirling in the mirror of your mother's bedroom closet door.

LOU   I didn't do it every day.

MRS. WILLARD   Take me back, Lou, to that little boy you were.

LOU   There's nothing else to tell.

MRS. WILLARD   Who are you saving it for?

LOU   She had this one really beautiful big skirt. It was red with white flowers embroidered on it—camellias, she told me. It was from Mexico and when they had parties she wore it with a white off-the-shoulder blouse. The blouse was from Mexico, too. My mother had beautiful shoulders; she loved to show them. Anyway, this skirt was the biggest skirt you ever saw. Perfect for flaring, but she never made it flare. She just wore it like any skirt. My mother never twirled.

MRS. WILLARD   Did you ever ask her to?

LOU   Of course not.

MRS. WILLARD   Why not?

LOU   That's not the sort of thing you can ask your mother.

MRS. WILLARD   It seems perfectly simple to me. "Mom, I finished my homework. Now will you twirl for me?"

LOU   You obviously don't have a son.

MRS. WILLARD   That's an interesting presumption.

LOU   Do you?

MRS. WILLARD   Finish your story.

LOU   Did you?

MRS. WILLARD   I'm waiting.

LOU You had to twirl really fast to make this skirt flare out. I mean, it was made for grown-ups. I was too little to turn fast enough to make it really flare. I could only make it flare a little bit. Sometimes I felt it was pulling me down, like I would drown in it, so I would close my eyes and twirl very slowly and pretend it was flaring out.

MRS. WILLARD Did you ever, in all your twirling, achieve full flair?

LOU Why are you humiliating me?

MRS. WILLARD That was not my intention. I feel very close to you. Cancer makes for great empathy, Lou. If what you told me was the truth—

LOU Of course it's the truth!

MRS. WILLARD If what you told me was the truth—

LOU You think I'd make something like that up?

MRS. WILLARD If what you told me was the truth—

LOU Of course it was the truth!!

MRS. WILLARD Then why are you getting so angry?

LOU Because it was the truth.

MRS. WILLARD If what you told me was the truth, I'm touched. The truth is the greatest gift we can give each other, and we so seldom do. Thank you, Lou.

LOU You're welcome.

MRS. WILLARD Now twirl for me, Lou.

LOU You've already seen me.

MRS. WILLARD   I watched in mockery because I didn't know how much you wanted love. This time I will watch with compassion. Twirl for me, Lou, and I'll give you my theatre.

LOU   Do I have to?

MRS. WILLARD   I'm giving you my theatre. You're giving me yourself. (*She makes a gesture for him to begin.*) Pretend you're alone. Close your eyes. Remember what it was like to be all alone with your dreams. Put your arms out. That's right. Listen for the music. Now start, Lou. Slowly, slowly. (*She hums the Tchaikovsky ballet music from before.*) Beautiful, that's beautiful, Lou, don't stop.

Lou has begun to twirl, slowly, his eyes closed, his arms out by his sides.

MRS. WILLARD (*cont.*)   The second string . . . and there *is* a second string, Lou, and you're the only one who will understand this . . . the second string. . . . Are you listening, Lou?

Lou nods and twirls.

MRS. WILLARD (*cont.*)   The second string is this: When the time comes, when the pain is too much, you will kill me. That's all, Lou. Just kill me.

Lou stops twirling and looks at Mrs. Willard, who begins to convulse with pain. She lets out a long moan, then stifles it.

MRS. WILLARD (*cont.*)   That's right, twirl, Lou, twirl! How do you like your new theatre? Isn't it beautiful?

The lights are fading.

End of Act One

ACT TWO

Arnold and Jessie are kissing. Jessie pulls away.

JESSIE Wait, I thought I heard something. They must be here somewhere. Her car's still out front.

ARNOLD Ssshhh.

Arnold kisses her again.

JESSIE I wish you hadn't lost your temper with her.

ARNOLD She's an easy woman to lose it with. Kiss me.

He kisses her again.

JESSIE I'm still hoping after Lou talks to her, she'll change her mind about the theatre.

ARNOLD Will you shut up about this place and let me tell you how much I love you?

JESSIE I know.

ARNOLD I love you, Jess. I want to marry you. I want you to be my wife and a mother to my boys. I ache with this love, it's so strong. I'm not going to go on like this, Jessie. I want you to tell him.

JESSIE I can't.

ARNOLD Then I will.

JESSIE You don't have to. He must know.

ARNOLD How could he know? We've been so goddamn discreet I forget we're having an affair half the time. One night you're giving me a prop list for *Snow White;* the next, we're making love and I'm hoping the boys can't hear us.

JESSIE I would die if they did, Arnold.

ARNOLD I don't know what I am anymore, Your TD or your lover. It's very confusing.

JESSIE He knows. He has to know. I'm not that good an actress. I come home from your place and I must reek of you.

ARNOLD I'd respect him more if he acted like he knew. Something to show he cares I'm fucking you. Maybe I should punch him out—to show him *I* care I'm fucking you.

JESSIE I hate that word.

ARNOLD I want you to leave him, Jessie, and be with me.

JESSIE You don't leave someone just because you're sleeping with someone else.

ARNOLD It's a pretty good reason, Jess. At least my wife thought so.

JESSIE You don't leave a life you've built with someone just like that.

ARNOLD You do for a better one. Jess, we could be so happy.

JESSIE How could we be happy, knowing what we'd done to him?

ARNOLD He'll get over it.

JESSIE Lou wouldn't.

ARNOLD People get over things. It's human nature. I got over Carol. Jesus, Jessie, these are our lives I'm talking about.

JESSIE I can't just leave him.

ARNOLD You can't or you won't?

JESSIE Don't give me an ultimatum.

ARNOLD I love you, Jessie. I want to make you happy.

This time, she kisses him.

JESSIE Ida and her friend are right next door. They'll see us.

IDA'S VOICE (*from somewhere in the theatre*) Ida and her friend already have. We tried to make a noise.

Jessie and Arnold break apart as Ida and Toby come to the stage.

TOBY We just ate the world's worst cheeseburger, and we eat a lot of cheeseburgers on tour. I think it had nuts in it.

ARNOLD I could have told you where to go.

TOBY The French fries were pretty good, though.

JESSIE How long have you been there?

IDA Ma, I'm not judging.

JESSIE Children are always judging.

TOBY It's cool, Mrs. . . .

JESSIE It's Jessie.

TOBY My mother has a boyfriend, Jessie. He's a state trooper. He stopped her for speeding on the New England Turnpike and before you knew it they were going at it like two teenagers.

IDA Toby, chill. Where's Lou?

JESSIE Somewhere with Mrs. Willard, we assume.

ARNOLD I love your mother, Ida, and I believe she loves me.

IDA So what's the problem?

JESSIE There is no problem.

ARNOLD She thinks she has to stay with Lou and his goddamn theatre.

JESSIE It's your goddamn theatre, too. It's not that simple, Ida.

IDA All right, I think we need some serious girl talk here. Scram, Toby.

JESSIE Ida!

TOBY I am your daughter's complete doormat, she's walking all over me, like all the time, but I'm in love with her and I'm happy and isn't that the purpose of life? To be happy?

ARNOLD You hear that, Jessie?

TOBY That wasn't me, sir. That was the Buddha.

ARNOLD (*taking his arm*) That's good enough for me. Come on, maybe your girlfriend can talk my girlfriend into some sense. We'll be in the basement.

TOBY That was a trick iron maiden I saw down there, right?

ARNOLD I don't know. I'll let you get in, and we'll find out.

TOBY Cool.

They go beneath the stage.

IDA You two make wild love his kids can hear?

JESSIE God, I hope not. I'm like their soccer mom.

IDA It's cool, someone thinking your mother is sexy. How long have you two been at it?

JESSIE Almost three years and I wish you wouldn't put it like that. I feel like such a tramp.

IDA Ma, you couldn't be a tramp if you tried.

JESSIE Someone was bound to find out. Better you than anyone.

IDA Does Lou know?

JESSIE He asked me once. I was sewing a costume for *Pinocchio* and he said, "Are you having an affair with Arnold?" and I said, "Of course not," without missing a stitch. He's never mentioned it again.

IDA It's pretty obvious something's up.

JESSIE It's the way I behave with Arnold, isn't it?

IDA No, it's more the way Lou doesn't behave with you.

JESSIE How do you mean?

IDA He's gay, right?

JESSIE I hate that word. Lou is a lot of things. He's good, he's fun, he's—

IDA I'm not saying he's not all those things.

JESSIE It's a good relationship.

IDA But you need Arnold, too.

JESSIE Sometimes, yes, I do. I'm not very proud of myself.

IDA Ma, I don't blame you. If Lou's fooling around, why shouldn't you be?

69

JESSIE Lou doesn't do that.

IDA How do you know?

JESSIE He gave me his word.

IDA And you believe him?

JESSIE Yes; it's called trust.

IDA No, it's called denial. It's what men do, straight or gay. They go where their dicks take them.

JESSIE Lou is nothing like your father.

IDA No, I doubt I'll ever come home from school and find him screwing your best friend.

JESSIE I'm sure you'll make another hit song out of it if you do.

IDA What else am I supposed to write about, if not my life?

JESSIE *Lies My Mother Taught Me.* I suppose it's a good album title if you're not the mother. You didn't even bother to change the names.

IDA No one knows who you are.

JESSIE I do. It's a good thing we'd moved upstate. I was mortified.

IDA I'm sorry.

JESSIE It's a little late for that, honey.

IDA You'll be happy to know the new CD is about the future: life after rehab.

JESSIE And it's called *The Curse of an Broken Heart*?

IDA I still have a lot of issues.

JESSIE So do I. I don't rub everyone's noses in them. I keep them to myself.

IDA I'm a creative artist. You're just a reproductive one.

JESSIE What the hell is that supposed to mean?

IDA You've spent your life saying lines that were written by someone else.

JESSIE I'm sorry but that's what actors do, Ida. It's called the script.

IDA I speak in my own voice.

JESSIE That's wonderful. Just leave me out of it. And while we're at it, I don't understand your need to shock people.

IDA I don't understand yours to please them. Wake up and smell the coffee.

JESSIE I smell it every morning, Ida. Don't come home and tell me what's wrong with my life; I don't need my druggie daughter for that. I'm not the one on the front page of those newspapers and magazines at the checkout stand at the A&P.

She has begun to cry.

IDA We got something all turned around. I came home to make amends to you.

JESSIE I don't want your amends.

IDA I have to make them. It's part of the program. I need some closure.

JESSIE Don't make us *Oprah*, honey. Just talk to me.

IDA I'm trying. You're not making it any easier.

71

JESSIE I was way out of bounds with that druggie remark.

IDA Thank you. Yes, you were.

JESSIE It must have been terrible what you've been through.

IDA It was. I should be dead.

JESSIE Don't say that.

IDA If you don't believe me, ask Toby. He's the reason I'm alive. You treat someone like shit and they're still there for you.

JESSIE He loves you, Ida.

IDA Actually, I was talking about you.

JESSIE You're still my little girl. You always will be.

IDA I'd like to help you and Lou out if you'll let me.

JESSIE We don't want anything from you, honey. We're fine. Live a good life, be happy. You heard your boyfriend. He's very intelligent. He just seems otherwise.

IDA I'm gonna make the old bitch an offer she can't refuse and buy this place for you.

JESSIE We wouldn't take it, Ida.

IDA It would be a tax write-off for me. You know how the Rolling Stones have that place in the Caribbean where they work on their next albums and get ready for their tours?

JESSIE No, not really, honey.

IDA This would be my place like that. A total deduction. My accountant will be so happy.

JESSIE Are you pregnant?

IDA   Why do mothers always think their daughters are pregnant?

JESSIE   Are you?

IDA   I just found out.

JESSIE   That's wonderful. What does Toby say?

IDA   I haven't told him.

JESSIE   Why not?

IDA   He'll want me to have it.

JESSIE   And you don't?

IDA   I'm not sure yet. I'm scared I'll be a bad mother or that he won't love me.

JESSIE   He?

IDA   Or she.

JESSIE   Everyone feels that way. Your father didn't want me to have you.

IDA   You never told me that.

JESSIE   He said he didn't want to be a father. It turned out he didn't want to be a husband, either.

IDA   Am I the reason he left you?

JESSIE   No, honey. Your father had trouble being a human being.

IDA   To think that you can come that close to not being born!

JESSIE   Life is wonderful and sometimes it's not. That's all we're trying to show the kids at Captain Lou's.

IDA That's a lot, Ma.

JESSIE Children can handle it. It's the adults who sometimes can't. You should see me after a performance of *A Christmas Carol*. No Mrs. Cratchit has cried more when Scrooge comes through the door with the goose than your mother. Lou breaks my heart in that scene every Christmas.

IDA You were a good actress.

JESSIE Thank you.

IDA No, really good. I don't know why I could never tell you that.

JESSIE Well, you just did.

IDA We're gonna have to get back soon. Come on, if I can't buy you a theatre, at least let me treat you to a grilled cheese and bacon next door.

JESSIE I bet that's where they are.

IDA "With the mustard on the cheese *before* you grill it, please." See? I remember.

JESSIE Actually, I've moved on to BLTs on toasted rye, hold the mayo.

IDA As long as you're not a vegan.

JESSIE That magazine said *you* were one.

IDA I was until Toby. He reminded me that eating is supposed to be fun.

JESSIE Can I ask you something, Ida? It's killing me.

IDA Go ahead.

JESSIE Did you really have an affair with Sting?

IDA Of course not.

JESSIE I was very jealous when I read that. What about Ricky Martin?

IDA Get real!

They go. The stage is bare a moment. A gust of wind blows across it. Curtains stir in it. We hear voices: distant, from the past: a bit of Shakespeare, someone singing, an audience roaring in laughter at a comic.

For a moment the theatre is alive again with all the voices and sounds of its past.

All this fades as Lou and Mrs. Willard return.

LOU I don't understand, why does it have to be today?

MRS. WILLARD I'm ready. I woke up this morning and I could see it was going to be a perfect summer's day, so I decided it would be my last. That delicious breeze off the lake was the clincher. It doesn't get any better than this. Besides, there's a lovely symmetry. Your birthday, my deathday. My life for your dreams.

LOU You say it with a sneer.

MRS. WILLARD There was no sneer.

LOU There was a sneer.

MRS. WILLARD Well, maybe a tiny one. I don't like children and I don't like the theatre. Put them together and I suppose a sneer is inevitable.

LOU Why me of all people?

MRS. WILLARD I think it was preordained. The chance meeting at the cinema with your wife, the same cancer. Besides, how many people would want a place like this?

LOU I haven't said I'm going to do it.

MRS. WILLARD Now tell me about your cancer.

LOU I told you: I don't like to talk about it.

MRS. WILLARD Fair enough. What meds are you on?

LOU I leave all that to Jessie. She's very tight with the doctors. What meds are you on?

MRS. WILLARD Tanqueray, Beefeaters, Gordon's. It's called the English gin protocol.

LOU Maybe you do have a sense of humor.

MRS. WILLARD I don't trust what the doctors prescribe, but I do know where a fifth of gin is going to take me, every time. Gin is reliable. All their chemo and radiation are not. (*long beat*) You live your whole life in fear of it and then one day they tell you you have it.

LOU It's not fair.

MRS. WILLARD I didn't say that. It's not fair, of course, but you don't have to rub it in. What will you miss the most?

LOU Jessie.

MRS. WILLARD That's a good answer.

LOU You?

MRS. WILLARD This, just breathing. (*another beat*) I'll tell you something that's not fair: You still have all your hair.

LOU It's a matter of time.

She takes off her wig.

MRS. WILLARD Well, don't make a face. I don't look that awful. So what are you going to do with your theatre?

Lou just looks at her.

MRS. WILLARD (*cont.*) This is what a dying woman looks like. Get over it. I asked you a question: What are you going to do with your theatre?

LOU Put on plays, what else?

MRS. WILLARD "Put on plays." That sounds so wishy-washy. I want my theatre to be a place that matters. I want my theatre to change lives.

LOU We're only a children's theatre, but I think *Cinderella* changes lives. I think *Sleeping Beauty* is a matter of life and death. I think if we reach one child, just one, it will be worth everything.

MRS. WILLARD You really believe that?

LOU It's what keeps me alive, Mrs. Willard.

MRS. WILLARD You need a martini.

LOU I don't drink.

MRS. WILLARD Well, I do. Edward!

LOU And I don't murder old ladies, either.

MRS. WILLARD Old? Now I'm insulted. Cunt I could live with.

LOU The courts are going to call it murder.

MRS. WILLARD The courts aren't going to know anything about it. My doctor will sign a certificate of death that will

77

say I died the way I was expected to die—the way you're going to die, Lou—and that will be that. That's all death is, really: a matter of that being that.

LOU   Why can't you just die like you're supposed to?

MRS. WILLARD   The way I'm supposed to die is in agony. Why would you wish me that? Somebody told me I would be in good company when I was gone: Shakespeare, Beethoven, someone called Jimi Hendrix. It sounds like a surreal dinner party. I'd be happy to meet Carole Lombard and Eleanor Roosevelt and leave it at that.

Edward appears.

EDWARD   Remember the little boy whose dog had run away?

MRS. WILLARD   Skip you said his name was.

EDWARD   Well, they found him.

MRS. WILLARD   They found Skip's dog! That's a relief.

EDWARD   They found Tiger in a box cut up into little pieces. Some sick mind had—you don't want to know what they did to that dog. Poor little Skip, he's heartbroken.

LOU   Where did this happen? Right here in town?

EDWARD   Of course not. Nothing ever happens in this town.

MRS. WILLARD   You know how the soaps upset you, Edward. Edward is addicted to soap operas.

EDWARD   When the soaps start getting ugly like everything else is when I stop watching them. They're supposed to be an oasis of fantasy in a world gone mad with violence.

LOU   Then you should come to our theatre.

EDWARD   I saw a play once. I didn't like it. *Hedda Gabler.* I would have shot her long before she shot herself.

MRS. WILLARD   You got off lucky, Edward. For me, it was an uncut *Peer Gynt.* I thought I'd died and gone to hell. Guess what? I had.

EDWARD   I prefer sports. Not all sports, contact sports. Body-to-body. Do you wrestle?

LOU   I'm sorry?

EDWARD   Do you like to wrestle? I'm always looking for someone to wrestle with. Put on our singlets and see who's top dog, know what I mean?

MRS. WILLARD   Edward wrestled for . . . what school was it, Edward?

EDWARD   SUNY Binghamton.

MRS. WILLARD   Not Yale?

EDWARD   SUNY Binghamton.

MRS. WILLARD   Your job resume said it was Yale.

EDWARD   It was SUNY Binghamton. So do you? Wrestle?

LOU   I'm retired.

EDWARD   I don't mean professionally. I meant for fun.

LOU   Oh, fun. No, I have Jessie for that.

MRS. WILLARD   That was a joke, Edward.

EDWARD   'Cause if you ever want to go a few rounds. I can lend you a singlet.

LOU   Thank you, Edward.

EDWARD   Call me Eddie. Mrs. Willard is the only one who calls me Edward. I look great in a singlet. You got to be a man to be able to wear a singlet, you know what I mean?

LOU   Absolutely.

EDWARD   You'd look great in a singlet. Another, Mrs. Willard?

MRS. WILLARD   Go easy on the vermouth this time.

EDWARD   I went easy.

MRS. WILLARD   Then go easier. Are you sure you won't join me, Lou?

LOU   A beer. Can he do a beer?

EDWARD   Yes, I think he can do a beer.

LOU   I'm sorry.

EDWARD   In a glass, Lou?

MRS. WILLARD   Of course in a glass. SUNY Binghamton rears its ugly head.

He goes.

LOU   I'm not used to servants. They make me very nervous.

MRS. WILLARD   I've always felt Edward was on the verge of great violence himself. Take away his soap operas and none of us are safe! Of course, you hire someone from the Ten Most Wanted List in the local post office . . . ! That was a joke, Lou.

LOU   I know. I've stopped biting.

MRS. WILLARD   Are you attracted to him?

LOU   No.

MRS. WILLARD   I am. The thought of it, I mean, the memory of making physical love. The reality is something else. No one wants to fuck you when you're old and gray, Lou. That's a bitter pill to swallow.

LOU   Why did you ask me that?

MRS. WILLARD   It was a relatively direct question. They're generally the best kind. *Are* you?

LOU   It wouldn't matter: I don't think Edward is attracted to me.

MRS. WILLARD   I don't think Edward is attracted to either one of us. It's his loss, not ours. Tell me about your wife.

LOU   Jessie's not my wife. We just tell people we're married.

MRS. WILLARD   Why?

LOU   A small town, working with children, the Caesar's wife thing.

MRS. WILLARD   Well, your Calpurnia is fucking someone else.

LOU   I don't like that word.

MRS. WILLARD   I don't like it either but we all seem to use it.

LOU   She's fucking our technical director. I'm sure there's a joke there somewhere.

MRS. WILLARD   Shall we put our heads together and look for it, Lou?

LOU   It will be on me, whatever it is. Let's not.

81

MRS. WILLARD   Does Mr. Salt have a green card?

LOU   It's Chalk.

MRS. WILLARD   Don't be tedious. We could call Immigration
and have him deported.

LOU   My wife and I have an arrangement.

MRS. WILLARD   I hate that word, too. I had an arrangement
with Mr. Willard.

LOU   Did it work?

MRS. WILLARD   Of course not. They never do. My heart was
broken. Be warned: Yours will be, too. Does anyone hate
you, Lou?

LOU   I don't know. I hope not. Why?

MRS. WILLARD   It's a terrible feeling. What are you going to
use?

LOU   I'm sorry?

MRS. WILLARD   To off me.

LOU   That's a terrible expression. Where did you pick it up?

MRS. WILLARD   Watching television with Edward.

LOU   I didn't think people like you watched television. I
thought you drank champagne and went to the opera.

MRS. WILLARD   I loathe the opera. Unattractive, overweight
people.

LOU   Not all of them.

MRS. WILLARD   I'm talking about the audience. People
spending much too much money to watch other

unattractive, overweight people singing ad nauseam about unrequited love. Of course it's unrequited. Have you had a good look at yourself, Pagliacci? You too, Madame Butterball. You got the champagne right. I like to settle down with some Dom Pérignon and an iced bowl of beluga and watch an episode of *American Idol*. When you're as sick as I am, you'll be grateful for such small pleasures. I leave the *Ring Cycle* for people who don't have a clue what real life is all about.

A sudden spasm of pain leaves her speechless.

MRS. WILLARD (*cont.*)   I think it's beginning, the final agony.

Edward returns with a glass of beer.

EDWARD   Budweiser Light. You look like you could lose a little around the middle.

LOU   The story of my life, Eddie.

MRS. WILLARD   Edward has a magnificent physique.

EDWARD   Used to, maybe. It's all gone to flab.

MRS. WILLARD   What's flab to you is rock-hard to everyone else.

EDWARD   Six percent body fat. My goal is zero. Put your hand here.

LOU   That's all right.

EDWARD   Put your hand here.

LOU   Really, I—

MRS. WILLARD   Put your hand there, Lou, or we'll be here all day.

LOU (*Lou puts his hand on Edward's abs.*)   Very impressive.

MRS. WILLARD   Edward was Mr. Vermont.

EDWARD   She makes it sound like a big deal.

MRS. WILLARD   It is, Edward.

EDWARD   If you're from Vermont. I'm from New Jersey. We got a lot of physical culturists in New Jersey, so I entered a competition in Vermont.

MRS. WILLARD   That's cheating.

EDWARD   You're not making me feel any better about it, Mrs. Willard. All right, you can take your hand away now, Lou. Have you two come to an agreement yet?

LOU   He knows?

MRS. WILLARD   Lonely rich old women tell their drivers everything.

LOU   Then get *him* to do it.

MRS. WILLARD   I tried.

EDWARD   Just because I look like a thug doesn't mean I'm gonna act like one.

MRS. WILLARD   Besides, I've entrusted Edward with all necessary documents to transfer the property to you.

Another spasm of pain wracks her.

MRS. WILLARD (*cont.*)   I was wrong, Lou, it's *begun,* the final agony. Help me, Edward, I want to get ready.

LOU   I won't do it. Mrs. Willard, I think you love the theatre.

MRS. WILLARD   I don't want the theatre; I want oblivion. I'm dying, Lou, and so are you. That's all it comes down to, on stage or off. Tell your children that.

Mrs. Willard and Edward go as Arnold returns from beneath the stage.

ARNOLD   I left Toby exploring the simple wonders of a snow machine. All that money they must have and he's never made it snow on an audience just by turning the crank of a drum filled with newspaper. What's the matter, Lou?

LOU   Mrs. Willard wants to give me her theatre.

ARNOLD   That's wonderful, Lou. What did you say? What did you do?

LOU   There are strings.

ARNOLD   She wants you to produce this bloody awful play she's written about Joan of Arc and she wants to play Joan. Do it! We'll use real logs and burn her at the stake at its one and only performance. And then it will be business as usual and straight on to Dreamland.

LOU   Is Jessie going to leave me?

ARNOLD   I've asked her to.

LOU   She's all I have.

ARNOLD   She's all I have, too.

LOU   Do you love her?

ARNOLD   Very much.

LOU   Does she love you?

ARNOLD   I think she does.

LOU What are we going to do?

ARNOLD I told Jessie we should duke it out.

LOU I should have seen this coming. I thought we were so safe, Jess and I, with our little theatre.

ARNOLD Sooner or later someone turns on the work lights and it's just a place like any other. All the magic and illusion are gone and the real world bites us in the ass.

LOU Why don't I know that?

ARNOLD You're not supposed to: You're an artist. But you'd be better off if you did, my friend. Now, do you want me to pick up next week's programs or will you? I can swing by the printers on my way to work.

LOU Don't take Jessie away from me, please, Arnold.

Jessie returns.

JESSIE I just had the best BLT ever. Chat 'n' Chew has a new cook—am I interrupting something?

ARNOLD We're discussing whether we should do *Treasure Island* or revive *Old King Cole* next season.

JESSIE My vote is for *Old King Cole*. The costumes are done and I can get an early start on my sewing for *Little Women*.

ARNOLD You're outvoted, Lou.

JESSIE What was Mrs. Willard's proposal?

LOU I'll explain later.

Ida and Toby return.

IDA We're gonna have to head back.

JESSIE Already?

86

IDA   Things go haywire when Toby's not around. The outfield speakers have all shorted.

JESSIE   You just got here.

IDA   Next time we'll stay, I promise.

Toby has pulled an old drop cloth off a tall, unfamiliar standing object. A prop stage guillotine is revealed.

TOBY   Is this what I think it is? Whoa, does somebody want to give me a hand with this?

Arnold helps Toby place the guillotine center stage.

JESSIE   I haven't seen one of those since high school. I played Madame Defarge. I sat there, knitting furiously, trying to upstage the female lead, and wishing the great line was mine: "I regret I have only one life to give for my country."

ARNOLD   A stirring performance but the wrong revolution, Jess. I think you mean, "It is a far, far better thing I do."

Ida joins Toby at the guillotine.

IDA   So what's up, lover?

TOBY   Ida, I'm having one of my rock fantasy visions! This could be you in this thing. This could be so sick, Eye.

IDA   I want better than sick. I want deformed.

TOBY   You finish the regular show with "Stepping on My Heart."

IDA   Right.

TOBY   The crowd is going crazy. I-da, I-da, I-da! The guys tear into "Dead End" but suddenly they trans-ish into something nobody's ever heard before, a new song. The song is called "Roadkill." It's about how we're all gonna

87

get it, sooner or later, how we're all just so much roadkill to the gods. It's right out of *King Lear.* "As flies to wanton boys, are we to the gods. They kill us for their sport."

IDA   I think I know where you're going with this. I start singing.

TOBY   This is so bent.

IDA   And while I'm singing. . . .

TOBY   This thing comes up from under the stage. "Oooooo," everybody goes, I can just hear 'em! "Ooooo." Now I bring out a basket. What's he gonna do with it? I put it down in front of the guillotine. "Oh my God," they're going, "oh my God." Take it, Eye!

IDA   I get on my knees and put my head in. People are freaking out.

TOBY   The stadium is in total frenzy.

IDA   I'm still singing when the blade falls. The crowd screams. Half of them shut their eyes. I'm still singing from deep inside the basket. Toby takes my head out of the basket and I'm still singing.

TOBY   She's still singing.

IDA   He holds it up, high over his head. I'm still singing.

TOBY   It's Ida's head. Get it? It's a hologram. She's still singing.

IDA   The lights begin to fade. Total darkness. The show is over. I'm still singing!

TOBY   She's still singing.

IDA   Fucking A!

TOBY   And people wonder why I love this woman. She's a genius. A rock 'n' roll genius.

LOU   It sure beats Rumpelstiltskin! If this is what we're competing with for the next generation's attention!

IDA   So how does this thing work?

TOBY   Get in, I'll show.

JESSIE   You will not, Toby! Use something else.

IDA   That is the same voice that wouldn't let me go swimming for one full hour after I'd eaten.

Toby finds a mop and puts it into the guillotine.

LOU   Ida, you're upsetting your mother.

IDA   Everything upsets my mother.

TOBY   Okay, pretend this is you, Eye. You're singing, the blade is rising, higher and higher, people are freaking. You're still singing when the blade drops. . . .

The blade drops and "decapitates" the broom head from the handle.

IDA   You would have fucking killed me!

TOBY   I don't know what went wrong.

ARNOLD   It's the oldest trick in the book. Here, I'll show you.

JESSIE   You will not. I'm putting my foot down this time. I said, leave it, Arnold! God gave you a voice, a beautiful voice, Ida. You don't need this crap.

IDA   It's what people want. It's all theatre.

JESSIE   I don't know where you got such disdain for everything you were raised on. If nothing else, I thought I'd taught you theatre is love.

IDA   That's why this place is empty and we're playing to a sold-out arena.

JESSIE   It's not a contest, Ida.

IDA   The glory of the theatre!

JESSIE   Yes! If these walls could talk, they would shame us with their eloquence. There were flights of the imagination here, journeys of the heart. If only I had a magic wand! It would all come back and it would all be wonderful again.

IDA   Dream on, Ma, it's not going to happen. It's over, your theatre.

JESSIE   What Lou and I do matters.

IDA   How can it matter if nobody comes?

JESSIE   I don't know, it just does.

ARNOLD   Well said, Jess.

TOBY   Ida's going to sing for thousands and thousands of people in a couple of hours. Some will have come hundreds of miles to see her. Others will have saved up for weeks. They'll buy her CDs and T-shirts because they want to take some piece of her home with them. I don't think she knows how she touches and changes them. I don't think you do either, Mrs. Nuncle.

JESSIE   Take good care of my daughter, Toby.

TOBY   I'm trying to.

IDA   You take care of me fine.

Toby holds her until she pulls away from him. Hugs and handshakes as Toby and Ida make their departure.

JESSIE We're going to want a pair of tickets for Sunday.

IDA Comps?

JESSIE Yes, comps. I'm your mother, for Christ's sake. (*to Lou*) I can see who she's taking after and you're not even her father. "Comps?" (*calling after Ida*) And if you were planning on singing any songs about me, don't. Especially "Crack Momma."

Ida and Toby have disappeared up the aisle of the theatre.

JESSIE It looks like I'm going to be a grandmother, Lou.

LOU That's wonderful, Jess.

JESSIE Old Mother Hubbard at last.

ARNOLD If you don't need me anymore, I'm going to be heading over to the theatre. They're having trouble with the Fairy Godmother's coach. Cinderella won't make it to the ball tonight if I don't.

LOU Thanks, Arnold.

ARNOLD No problem. And thank you, Jessie, for setting me straight.

JESSIE How do you mean?

ARNOLD I thought this was about a woman who was trying to choose between two men—both willing, both able, both very much in love with her—and I fooled myself into thinking that which one she chose had anything to do with me. Wrong play, Arnold! She was always yours, Lou! I don't think I even came close. You're a lucky man. Early curtain tonight, folks, don't forget. I'll pick up those programs on the way, Lou. Just close the door behind you when you're through.

He goes.

LOU   Are you okay?

JESSIE   I'm always okay. I've been okay my entire life. I would like to be great, just once. I would like to be wonderful.

LOU   Do you love him?

JESSIE   Sometimes I think I do.

LOU   I don't know what you see in him. Yes I do. He's a good man. Maybe he's got a brother in Brighton.

JESSIE   Be serious, Lou.

LOU   I am, Jess. What are we going to do?

JESSIE   We? I don't know what that word means anymore, Lou.

LOU   It means I love you, for one thing. Are you going to leave me?

JESSIE   Would you like me to?

LOU   How can you say that? I made you a promise.

JESSIE   I'm releasing you from it.

LOU   How little you know me, Jess.

JESSIE   Oh, I think I know you pretty well, Lou.

LOU   I've forgotten what it's like to be held.

JESSIE   I'll hold you.

LOU Really held.

JESSIE I know, I know.

LOU To be physically passionate with another person. To be loved that way, too.

JESSIE There's someone out there who will hold you the way you want to be held, Lou, but you're not going to find them at Captain Lou and Miss Jessie's. Maybe you're the one who wants to leave this relationship. Are you in love?

LOU Do I look like someone in love?

JESSIE I don't know what someone in love looks like anymore.

LOU You just saw one leave. Run after him, Jessie. I wouldn't blame you.

JESSIE I don't think he's coming back this time.

LOU You're stuck with me.

JESSIE Not stuck, Lou; never stuck.

LOU Lou and Jessie; Jessie and Lou. The Inconsolables.

Jessie puts her arms out to him.

JESSIE Come on, you're still my best partner.

LOU There's no music.

Jessie hums and they begin to slow-dance. They haven't forgotten their routine.

LOU *(cont.)* Romantic love and me have always been strangers. The kind of love we do plays about.

JESSIE *(It's all coming back.)* We were good. We still are.

93

LOU You were in this satin gown, white! All white and I was in a white satin top hat and tails. Did we both have canes or just me?

JESSIE Both. We both did.

They dance until:

LOU She wants to give us this place and enough money to bring it back to life.

JESSIE Why didn't you tell me?

LOU There's a condition.

JESSIE She wants it renamed for her! The Annabelle Willard Children's Theatre. Can I live with that? You bet I can.

LOU She wants me to kill her.

JESSIE What are you talking about?

LOU She's afraid of the pain. It's becoming too much and she wants me to kill her. Now! She's getting ready.

JESSIE I don't like this conversation, Lou.

LOU Neither do I, Jess.

JESSIE You told her you wouldn't even entertain such a thought?

LOU I'm just laying out the options, Jessie.

JESSIE There is no option.

LOU She's going to die anyway. I would just be helping her.

JESSIE It's called murder, Lou.

LOU   Not if the person asks you to do it. If I end up like her, who do you think I'm going to ask to put me out of my misery? Arnold?

JESSIE   That's different. I love you.

LOU   The way you loved your mother?

JESSIE   I loved my mother.

LOU   No you didn't, Jess.

JESSIE   She was still my mother. I did what I thought was right.

LOU   You took her off life support.

JESSIE   You saw how she was suffering, you were there.

LOU   I've seen how Mrs. Willard is suffering.

JESSIE   It's not the same thing. That was legal. This is murder.

LOU   I don't see the difference. Besides, all you got when your mother was gone was peace of mind—yours. We'd be doing this for something real.

JESSIE   My mother was real.

LOU   I won't do it if you tell me no.

JESSIE   She's an old woman. She doesn't know what she's saying.

LOU   She knows exactly what she's saying. A place that can change lives forever in exchange for a life that has already devoured itself in selfishness and bitterness greater than any cancer.

JESSIE   You really believe that, don't you?

LOU So do you, Jess, that's why we've stuck it out.

JESSIE What do you want, Lou?

LOU I want the theatre.

Mrs. Willard and Edward enter.

MRS. WILLARD I'm ready if you are, Lou. Where are the others?

LOU They've gone.

MRS. WILLARD Have you explained the situation?

LOU Yes. Now? Does it have to be right now?

MRS. WILLARD Yes, now, please, Lou. Edward, take the lady away.

EDWARD Thank you, Mrs. Willard. I didn't want to be here for this.

MRS. WILLARD I wasn't thinking about you, Edward. We have your blessing, Jessie?

JESSIE Is that important?

MRS. WILLARD To me, not at all. To your partner it should be of some consequence.

JESSIE We have callbacks tonight for *Snow White,* Lou.

LOU I know, Jess.

EDWARD Good-bye, Mrs. Willard. I didn't hate you.

Jessie and Edward are gone.

MRS. WILLARD She seems like a good person.

LOU She is.

MRS. WILLARD   I thought this pillow would do the trick. Edward found it on a prop table. *Othello,* last scene, smothering pillow. Who gets smothered in *Othello?*

LOU   His wife.

MRS. WILLARD   Why? Did she have cancer of the esophagus, too?

LOU   Othello thought she was unfaithful to him.

MRS. WILLARD   I hope that doesn't give you any ideas. I'd think you'd better stop with me.

LOU   How is the pain?

MRS. WILLARD   Unspeakable. You have a lot to look forward to.

LOU   There are sedatives.

MRS. WILLARD   There are so many things out there to take us away from where we really and truly are.

LOU   Like the theatre.

MRS. WILLARD   I won't be long. We can make small talk; I'm very good at it. The pain is coming more and more frequently, rather like labor pains.

LOU   Then you were or are a mother? There is or was a son? I knew it.

MRS. WILLARD   That isn't small talk. Are you going to re-cover the seats in red plush or blue? Marie Antoinette's private little playhouse at Versailles had blue plush-covered seats, I remember. *That* is small talk.

LOU   He's dead, isn't he?

MRS. WILLARD   Yes, he's dead. So what? So bloody what? British invective is so much more satisfying than ours. "So fucking what?" is just coarse.

LOU   He was an only child?

MRS. WILLARD   Thank God, yes. I couldn't bear to have lost two.

LOU   What happened?

MRS. WILLARD   I killed him.

LOU   I don't understand.

MRS. WILLARD   I smothered him with a pillow, like you're going to smother me.

The pain is very fierce.

MRS. WILLARD (*cont.*)   Not yet, not yet. I'll tell you when. I want you to name this theatre for him. That's another string! His name was Justin.

LOU   Justin.

MRS. WILLARD   Justin Makepeace Willard. It was an absurd name; his father insisted on it, for entirely selfish reasons. Let's not waste our time on them.

LOU   How old was he?

MRS. WILLARD   Young, very young. Little more than a year. We realized rather soon he would never see or hear. Then it became apparent his spinal column was not developing and he would never be able to support himself to walk or sit up, even. The brain wasn't developing either. There were no motor skills. Their dreadful term, not mine. It made him sound like a car. Instead, he was a vegetable.

They recommended a special home, hidden away somewhere in Maine, I believe, with unlimited visiting privileges. They said he might live to be a hundred.

LOU   How terrible for you. How terrible for anyone.

MRS. WILLARD   There wasn't much Mr. Willard and I could do but just stand there, looking down at him in his crib. Our vegetable didn't like to be picked up or held. One day my husband stepped out of the room, leaving me alone with him, and when Mr. Willard stepped back, Justin was gone.

LOU   I think I can understand.

MRS. WILLARD   And there you are, Lou, holding another pillow. That should appeal to your sense of drama.

LOU   You killed your son and now you want me to kill you.

MRS. WILLARD   It all comes home to roost, n'est-ce pas? I never liked people who said "n'est-ce que pas." I thought it was affected and now I say it all the time. God, what a terrible journey this is!

Her cry of pain is paralyzing this time.

LOU   Mrs. Willard, I don't have cancer.

MRS. WILLARD   Yes you do.

LOU   My wife told you a lie.

MRS. WILLARD   (*The pain is making her delirious. Delirious and vicious.*)   It wasn't a lie. You have cancer. Everyone has cancer, or they will. It's the human condition. We all have cancer and we're going to die. Now tell me about your dreams. I told you about my son, now tell me about your dreams.

99

The spasms of pain increase in intensity, making it more and more difficult for Lou to continue.

LOU   Well, for one thing, we're going to put on plays that make children confident about their future.

MRS. WILLARD   In the great theatrical tradition of lying to the audience, no matter how young.

LOU   Plays that teach them there is goodness and hope and love in the world.

MRS. WILLARD   Who loves you, Lou? Who ever loved you?

LOU   Plays that make them want to be better people.

MRS. WILLARD   Are you a better person, Lou?

LOU   Plays that make them feel they're not alone.

MRS. WILLARD   I am alone. I have always been alone. So are you. Everyone is alone when they least want to be. Kill me, goddamn it!

Lou begins to smother Mrs. Willard with the pillow. She begins to struggle, putting up a tremendous resistance. A violent, ugly struggle ensues.

When it is over, Lou throws the pillow far away from him.

Music. Tchaikowsky. The Sleeping Beauty.

At once, over the proscenium the words "Captain Lou and Miss Jessie's Magic Theatre for Children of All Ages" is spelled out in bright theatrical lights.

Lou looks up at it, then back at Mrs. Willard.

A beautiful new curtain falls in place, blocking Lou and Mrs. Willard from view.

The chandelier bursts into dazzling light. The theatre is ablaze in newfound glory.

The music builds to an appropriate climax suitable for such a gala occasion.

Jessie steps between the curtains, resplendent in her Fairy Godmother costume.

JESSIE Welcome to the grand opening of Captain Lou and Miss Jessie's Magic Theatre for Children of All Ages at the Justin Makepeace Willard Center for the Performing Arts. What can I tell you about Annabelle Willard? She loved the theatre. She loved children. She loved life.

Arnold sticks his head out from the wings.

ARNOLD We're almost ready back here.

JESSIE Arnold Chalk, our technical director. Come out here, Arnold.

Arnold is reluctantly brought out.

ARNOLD This is a great day for our community. No one deserves their own theatre more than Lou and Jessie Nuncle. I'm going to call places.

He disappears behind the curtain.

JESSIE I want to speak to the children in our audience. The rest of you can close your ears. What you are about to see is called a play. We actors will pretend that we are someone else but these people—Prince Charming, Cinderella, the Fairy Godmother—really do exist. Look around, you might be sitting next to one. I found my Prince Charming in the theatre. I love you, Captain Lou.

We hear three strong knocks from behind the closed curtain, as in classic European theatre.

JESSIE (*cont.*)   They're calling your Fairy Godmother to the stage. Let's begin. *Ssshhh!*

She disappears behind the curtain.

Lively music sets the scene as the curtain rises on a green forest.

The Fairy Godmother sits on a tree stump with her back to us.

Lou, dressed in a bunny costume, appears from behind a clump of bushes.

LOU   This is a good day to be a rabbit. The sun is shining, the sky is blue. This is a good day to be alive. Thump, thump, thump. Listen how my heart is beating. Look, it's the Fairy Godmother!

The Fairy Godmother turns and faces him. But instead of Jessie, Lou sees Mrs. Willard dressed as the Fairy Godmother.

MRS. WILLARD   What kind of plays are you going to do in my theatre?

Lou tries to recover himself and go on with the show.

ARNOLD (*from the wings*)   "Isn't she beautiful?"

LOU   Good plays.

MRS. WILLARD   What kind of lies are you going to tell?

ARNOLD   "Isn't she beautiful?"

LOU   No lies. I'm going to tell them the truth.

ARNOLD   That's not the cue.

Lou takes off his rabbit's head and moves down to the footlights.

LOU   Once upon a time there was a little boy.

We hear the distant strains of the Sleeping Beauty Waltz.

LOU (*cont.*)   His name was Louis Nuncle.

MRS. WILLARD   Go on, Lou, go on.

LOU   He was very much like you. This is for you,
Mrs. Willard, you and your son. It's for you, too, Jessie.
Thank you, Fairy Godmother.

The light fades on Mrs. Willard.

Lou remains in a spotlight.

He smiles: He knows what to do now.

*He closes his eyes, puts his arms out, and begins to twirl, very, very
slowly. His smile broadens. Music up as he continues to twirl.*

The lights are fading on Lou as he twirls to the music.

Blackout.

Terrence McNally won Tony Awards for Best Play for *Love! Valour! Compassion!* and *Master Class,* as well as Tony Awards for Best Book of a Musical for *Ragtime* and *Kiss of the Spider Woman.* In addition, *Love! Valour! Compassion!* won the Drama Desk, Outer Critics Circle, and New York Drama Critics' Circle Awards for Best Play. He also wrote the book for *The Full Monty* and *The Visit.* His other plays include *Corpus Christi,* which was named one of the best plays of 1998 by *Time* magazine; *The Stendhal Syndrome; A Perfect Ganesh; Lips Together, Teeth Apart; The Lisbon Traviata; Frankie and Johnny in the Clair de Lune;* and *It's Only a Play.* Earlier stage works include *Bad Habits, The Ritz, Where Has Tommy Flowers Gone?, And Things That Go Bump in the Night,* and the book for the musical *The Rink.* He has written a number of television scripts, including *Andre's Mother,* for which he won an Emmy Award. Mr. McNally has received two Guggenheim fellowships, a Rockefeller grant, a Lucille Lortel Award, and a citation from the American Academy of Arts and Letters. A member of the Dramatists Guild since 1970, Mr. McNally has been vice president since 1981. Terrence McNally was raised in Corpus Christi, Texas, in the 1950s.